BACK IN ACTION

BACK IN ACTION

AN AMERICAN SOLDIER'S STORY OF COURAGE, FAITH, AND FORTITUDE

CAPTAIN DAVID ROZELLE

Since 1947
REGNERY
PUBLISHING, INC.
An Eagle Publishing Company • Washington, DC

Library of Congress Cataloging-in-Publication Data

Rozelle, David.
  Back in action : an American soldier's story of courage, faith, and
fortitude / David Rozelle.
    p. cm.
  ISBN 0-89526-041-7
  1. Rozelle, David. 2. Iraq War, 2003—Personal narratives, American.
3. Amputees—United States—Biography. I. Title.
  DS79.76.R694 2005
  956.7044'342'092—dc22

                        2005000513

Published in the United States by
Regnery Publishing, Inc.
An Eagle Publishing Company
One Massachusetts Avenue, NW
Washington, DC 20001
Visit us at www.regnery.com

Distributed to the trade by
National Book Network
4720-A Boston Way
Lanham, MD 20706

Printed on acid-free paper

Manufactured in the United States of America

10 9 8 7 6 5 4 3 2 1

Books are available in quantity for promotional or premium use. Write to Director of Special Sales, Regnery Publishing, Inc., One Massachusetts Avenue, NW, Washington, DC 20001, for information on discounts and terms or call (202) 216-0600.

For Forrest.
May we win this war so that you will always know freedom.
And for Kim, who has always believed in me.

Contents

CHAPTER 1

The Price of Freedom

I T'S NOT HARD TO GET YOUR MIND FOCUSED for a mission when there's a price on your head. It was the day that would change my life forever, 21 June 2003, in Hit (pronounced "heat"), Iraq.

Just a few days before, my translator and I were smoking cigarettes and enjoying some hot tea, waiting with a few sheiks for our weekly situation meeting to begin. I was the de facto sheriff of Hit. As we waited for the rest of the sheiks to arrive, we would discuss the Iran–Iraq war. My translator had been a POW in the war, held for eleven years in an Iranian prison. He had been pressed into military service after his third year of medical school and served as an infantryman. As a POW, he found himself doing procedures in prison with no anesthesia, no sanitary rooms, and few medical instruments. His

techniques kept fellow prisoners alive, but were often brutal and crip-
pling. After getting out of prison, he decided to never practice medicine again. He was a good man, and was proud to be of service to those
who had freed him for the second time in his life.

After taking a long drag on one of my Marlboros, he looked over
at me and said in a low voice, "Captain, do not go on your mission
tonight."

I was surprised. "I always lead my men," I responded. "It's still
dangerous and I want to command on the ground."

He said, "Your men will be safe, but you will be attacked. If you
go, it may be your last mission."

"What the hell are you talking about?" I said angrily. In a loud
voice, so that the sheiks in the room could hear, I continued, "You're
not trying to threaten me, are you? I will destroy any man who attacks
me. Tell me who is saying these things—I'll arrest them today!"

He spoke to me carefully, in a low voice so that others couldn't
hear, trying to calm me: "Captain, there are men in town who are planning missions in our mosques, under the command of clerics here and
from Ar Ramadi. These men I do not know. But they are dangerous.
Some are from Iran, and some are from Syria. It's rumored that they
have offered $1,000 U.S. to any man who can kill you, the one who
rides in the vehicle with the symbols K6 on the side . . . the one who
always wears sunglasses. They recognize you as the leader, and as one
who is successful and powerful. . . . Please do not go tonight."

I responded out loud, "You spread the word: I am powerful and
I command many men. Out of respect for the people of Hit, I have yet
to bring my tanks into this city and show you my full combat capabil-

ities. Let the town know that the whereabouts of these terrorists must be reported in order to protect the innocent civilians of this city. I'm not afraid and I'm not threatened."

On our mission that night, we did arrest several suspicious people and killed two men who tried to attack our tanks with rocket-propelled grenades (RPGs). After such a wild night, we decided to stay out of the city for a few days. Unfortunately, we were giving the terrorists more time to prepare their next attack.

It was 1630 hours on the day of my final mission. I could tell when my men were ready because the sounds below changed from bolts charged and orders given during the final pre-combat inspection to laughter and tough talk. I never came down from my command post until I heard the distinctive sound of my high mobility multi-wheeled vehicle (Humvee), distinctive because each Humvee has its own pitch or hum. Upon hearing that sound, I knew that my windshield and binocular lenses were clean, my maps updated with the most current intelligence, my radios checked, and my personal security detachment was loaded, with weapons pointed outward. With so many antennae and barrels protruding, we must have looked like some strange oversized desert insect. But before I walked down to conduct my final inspection, I continued my tradition of kissing the picture of my wife, Kim, listening to the message she had recorded in the frame, and saying a short prayer to God to take care of my unborn child if I did not return.

I was "Killer 6," which is the code word for the leader of K Troop, 3rd Squadron, 3rd Armored Cavalry Regiment. I commanded 139 men, nine M1A2 main battle tanks, 13 M3A2 Cavalry fighting vehicles, two tracked vehicles carrying 120 mm mortar guns, three support tracked vehicles, and five wheeled vehicles.

Before heading out on the mission, I would walk the line of soldiers to look at their faces. It wasn't just to make a final inspection. They needed to see me confident and unafraid of our impending mission. We treated every mission the same, whether we were conducting a traffic control point (TCP) or were capturing terrorists. My men had to be ready for anything.

A few weeks earlier, my boss had informed me that now that we had "stood up" an entirely new police force, we had to train them in police work. This tasking was a V Corps requirement. I was excited about it, tired of conducting patrols where I spent most of my time watching over my shoulder. Training leads to confidence and job comfort. We had done something historic. Within weeks of the end of major combat operations, we had rearmed Iraqi soldiers and were now patrolling the streets with them. They certainly needed training, and training was our task for the night.

We had scheduled the first night of training to start at 1700 hours, as it promised to be cooler than midday. The sun did not set until 2030 or 2100 hours, so we had plenty of time to train. We had planned on teaching for two hours, which we knew would turn into three or four. We always planned twice the amount of time to do anything with local forces.

It was about 1640 hours when we finally headed out the gate of our compound. I was traveling with two of my Humvees, my own and an improvised gun-truck, and two military police (MP) Humvees. As I crossed through the wire at the lead of the convoy, I called my depar-

ture report to Squadron Operations Center and told my detachment
to lock and load their weapon systems.

On the squadron radio, I reported, "Thunder, this is Killer
6 . . . Killer is departing FOB Eden to Hit police academy, vicinity soccer stadium, with one officer and twenty-one enlisted."

Changing hand microphones, I immediately followed, "Killer,
this is Killer 6, lock and load your weapon systems and follow my
move."

After getting acknowledgments from the three vehicles following
me, I charged my 9 mm Beretta, watching as the bullet slipped easily
into the chamber. As was my custom, as a deterrent to possible wrong-
doers, I had my pistol outside the window in my right hand, and my
left inside on the Bible my father had given me just before deploying
to Iraq. Inscribed on the inside cover were the words, "Use it as a tour
guide," and in the back I had pasted a picture of my wife and me with
my parents, taken just after our deployment ceremony.

It was only about five miles from our Forward Operating Base
(FOB) to the town of Hit. Just before we reached the roundabout at
the north end of the city, I told my driver to turn left down a dirt road
we often used for observation by tanks at night.

I intended to avoid the roundabout in order to avoid detection
from any spies at the first intersection. The dirt road took us from one
paved road to another, and was only about two hundred meters in
length. Just as we reached the far side, I noticed that the gradual ter-
race that normally allowed easy access to the road was now steeper and
recently graded. Looking over the edge, I decided that the vehicles
could handle the drop and we started to ease over the ledge.

As we began rolling again, everything exploded.

My right front tire, just under my feet, detonated an anti-tank mine. The mine violently lifted the Humvee off the ground and set it back on the three remaining of four wheels. The blast was so powerful that most of it went out and up from the front tire, launching a door and tire a hundred meters away. Blinded by smoke and dust, I wasn't sure exactly what had just happened, but I knew we were either under attack by RPGs or artillery, or had struck a mine—and that I was injured.

I looked down and saw blood on my arms, and through my glasses I could see that my bulletproof vest seemed to have absorbed a lot of shrapnel. Everything was quiet. I could not speak. I was in terrible pain. I heard noises coming from my driver, screams of pain and fear. I was more confused than afraid.

Finally, I got my voice and asked, "Is everyone okay?"

My driver responded with more screams, and my translator simply gave me a crazy look.

We needed to get out of the Humvee. I began to pull at my left leg, but I couldn't get it free. My left foot was trapped under the firewall and heater. The right front portion of the vehicle's frame was now on the ground, so I set my right foot out into the sand to get some footing, in order to pull myself and my left leg free. But I couldn't get any footing.

I thought, "Fuck . . . Oh, God, I am hurt . . . I have to get out of here . . . Why aren't they shooting at me? We're trapped in a stationary vehicle . . . They've got me . . . Fuck, that hurts . . . Move, David, move now!"

It felt as if I were setting my right foot into soft mud or a sponge. I looked down to see blood and bits of bone squeezing out of the side of my right boot. I gave one big push and turned to dive into the arms of two brave men who ran selflessly into the minefield to save me.

My good friend and fiercest warrior, Sergeant First Class John McNichols, grabbed me and said, "Don't worry, sir, I've got you."

All I could do was look at the ground. I tried to use my feet, but neither one would bear my weight. I could hear First Sergeant Cobal sighing under the burden of my weight.

I looked into his eyes and said, "I can't walk. I'm fucked up."

Turning now to face Sergeant First Class McNichols, I said, "My feet are messed up."

Sergeant First Class McNichols smiled at me and said, "It's just a walk in the park, sir."

That was the last time I ever used my right foot.

CHAPTER 2

Sitting on the Border

I T WAS 27 APRIL 2003, THE NIGHT BEFORE we were to attack
north into Iraq. I was sitting on the back edge of my command
post on the border in Kuwait, cleaning my face with a wet wipe,
thinking about the long journey ahead. My lieutenants were filing into
the tent attached to the back of my command post. We had endured a
sandstorm all afternoon, which made planning and briefing difficult.
We finally got a break after six hours of hiding, but it was night now,
and everyone was tired and grim. Like everything else in war, it was
not how I had anticipated giving my last commands to my troops
before heading north. But since I was leaving in a few hours, it was my
only chance. As I began to call roll, I noticed a giant scorpion running
toward me from the edge of the tent. After screaming like a Chinese
opera singer and trying my best to stomp on it, I watched it simply

disappear into the sand just beneath me. Once the laughter died down, I said, "Men, this place is dangerous."

I was headed out in the morning, leaving the majority of my men to join me outside Baghdad a few days later. The commanders of each troop and company would travel north with their combat trains and establish a Tactical Assembly Area (TAA) southwest of Baghdad. We were to drive along assigned routes under the protection of the 3rd Infantry Division and assume defense of the TAA. In order to save money and wear on our tanks, they would be transported by heavy equipment transport trailers (HETTs) all the way to the outskirts of the TAA.

I had thought for months about what I would say to my men the night before we crossed into Iraq. I had heard stories about how some commanders acted the night prior to the attack into Kuwait during Operation Desert Storm. And for weeks, my older men told stories to the younger soldiers of what they had witnessed then. They laughed and remembered certain commanders with distaste. Some had prayed with their men, but prayer had seemed hopeless to most. A few leaders allowed their men time to write one last letter home to carry on their bodies, which seemed foreboding to me. I decided to not do anything different from any other night. So after I gave my orders I gave a few short words, unprepared, but from the heart.

"Men, we have worked for over a year together for these coming days. I am only sorry that we will not all cross into Iraq together. You know my intent and my expectations. I depend on you to lead with those in mind. I know there is still a lot of uncertainty about the weeks ahead, but know that whatever our mission is in Iraq, it will be important and historic. K Troop will lead the regiment with the honor that it has always had in combat. I am proud to lead you and to call you all friends. By the time you join me in Baghdad, we will have a few short days to prepare ourselves again for combat. Make sure you and every one of your men are ready." I stood and saluted, and proudly gave our troop motto, "Killers on the Warpath!"

After answering a few questions, we sat around and laughed at how dirty we were. You could no longer tell a man's race by his color, because we were all light brown. I tried to make the noise of the sand people from the original *Star Wars*. That brought some laughter, relief from tension, and a good change of subject. I had made the mistake, as some might say, of becoming friends with my platoon leaders and noncommissioned officers. I loved these men and would have loved to have said a prayer for their safety. But they knew all that and just kicked back and gave it to me as hard as I could give it to them. (Don't come in our circle with thin skin, because you won't last.)

I remember that afternoon mainly because of the storm. It was troubling me that one day before our assault north, I could barely see my hand in front of my face. I sat for hours, uncomfortably trying to just breathe. Yes, breathe. The air is so thick with sand and dust that it almost feels as if you could suffocate. I would soon learn how to live with this new feeling, but on such an important day, it felt especially constricting. One day earlier, I had had the opportunity to send about a third of my men to a nearby communications center to try to call home, and now I too longed to hear my wife's voice. I didn't want to talk to her, necessarily, because it would have been too difficult and too sobering. I had said goodbye back home, and that was to last until we were established in Iraq, victorious. I just wanted to hear her say "I love you," one more time. I thought about writing a letter, but it was impossible to explain what I felt. I couldn't imagine writing something that could be my last words. What does a man write to his wife the day before he rides into uncertainty? I did not have the words. So I sat, trying to breathe, imagining what our child would be like when I returned from this godforsaken place.

I spent that day walking the perimeter of my camp one last time. Although it was my obligation to ensure that the men were on watch, constantly improving their positions, and maintaining a sketch-card of their area of observation and fields of fire, it was also my chance to see every soldier. I talked to each of them, and tried to get a grasp of how each man was feeling. Some were excited and asked too many questions. Some were nervous, and even more nervous when I started asking them questions about various rules and procedures. It was the nervous ones I wanted to be sure their leaders had an eye on. Sure, we were all nervous. But to display it sometimes meant that it was something to worry about. I spent most of my time at each vehicle with the vehicle commanders. Some I might quiz, but most I just shared a coffee or cigarette with, talking about our wives or something silly about their kids. I love hearing about my soldiers' families, because they are the ones counting on my leadership. I knew each wife by name, and most of the kids' names.

At some point, we usually crawled around the tanks like spiders, inspecting load plans. The commanders of each vehicle were proud of the way they had repacked all their equipment again. It is typical in the Army to try to pack a hundred pounds of gear into a forty-pound sack.

Noncommissioned officers are the best at it; their creativity is amazing. Vehicles are designed and issued with load plans for all essential equipment. Almost every bit of space in each rack and space on the wall is labeled for something specific. So, to find room for televisions, radios, books, magazines, food, sodas, coffee machines, cigarettes, cots, and pictures of the family was a true feat of engineering.

Did I mention that I am a cavalryman? I joined the armored force because of a conversation I had prior to selecting my branch with Major General (Retired) Dennis Malcor, who told me a story about being a tanker in Vietnam. He said that he had just finished a battle in Vietnam and was headed back to base camp when he passed an infantry lieutenant who was emerging from the road. He stopped to talk, as passing officers on missions often do, to exchange info about routes, enemy, and even scores from games back home. He said that those infantry boys were out of water, food, and ammo. General Malcor filled up their canteens, gave them some food, and gave them a split of ammo. As he told me the story, he stopped and laughed, reflecting, " 'Poor bastards,' I thought as I reached down into my cooler and fished out a cold soda to enjoy." That day I decided never to be that "poor bastard."

For this mission though, I was leaving my M1A2 Abrams main battle tank behind. It was tough to leave my luxury items. I could afford to take only what I needed to survive for three days: one bag of nuclear biological chemical equipment, one rucksack with a week's worth of personal supplies, a chair, a cot, a box of maps, my weapons and pyro, and my load-bearing equipment with all its associated equipment. It is amazing how little I really needed, especially considering I

wouldn't change my clothes or wash myself for several weeks. In anticipation of the road march, I had given myself a sponge bath the night
before, and changed my underclothes for the first time since coming
to Kuwait two weeks earlier. That night it had rained. Then, as bad luck
would have it, we were blasted the next day with six hours of sandstorms. Although the sandstorms were a great nuisance, the rain was
the most troubling. It's extreme, coming in fast and reinforced by
wind. The droplets are really droplets of mud that do anything but
cleanse. If you are caught with your mouth open enough to breathe in
a raindrop, you are spitting dirt and grinding sand for hours. Nothing
is in moderation. Trying to stay clean became a hobby that I finally
gave up on.

My wheeled convoy of fifteen vehicles was lined up at dusk with
its lights shining across the open desert. For the first time that day, the
desert was peaceful. There was just a line of blue left on the horizon,
but enough to see the vastness of the earth. After all our training with
black-out drives (dim lighting for use with night-vision goggles), I
never imagined I would be sitting on the border of Iraq with my high
beams on. We had to move only a few miles to link up with the rest of
the squadron's wheels, but we all moved together, because the desert
is an easy place to get lost in at night—even for scouts, but they call it
"disoriented." There are horror stories of men getting lost in the desert
and continuing to drive under the delusion that they are going in the
right direction, only to later find themselves outside the reach of res-
cuers and dying of heatstroke. Even worse now would be to get mis-
taken for the enemy and killed. We even have an official acronym for
it: LID, Lost in the Desert. These may sound like campfire stories, but

it is enough to make folks think before they try to drive off on their own across all that sand. As the last bit of blue disappeared, with no other lights shining around the horizon and only the bright stars in the big sky, we looked like a space exploration mission, lined up to move out and discover the unknown. Indeed we were.

Before loading up in my Humvee, I had one last command to give. I told my driver to crank it up and join the front of our convoy. I ducked into my command post and found my executive officer, First Lieutenant Jon Kluck, "Mother Klucker." We had been through a lot in the last year and could know what was on the other's mind simply by reading each other's expressions. I found him, as I often do, holding two radios in one hand and updating the map board with the other. My scouts have ten kilometers of frontage, with tanks five kilometers apart and three kilometers behind. The field trains, which are our service support vehicles, can be as far as ten kilometers behind. Unlike an infantry officer, I can't just stand up and see my forces and how they are arrayed. I depend on concise reports from my lieutenants and platoon sergeants. My executive officer processes them and "paints the picture" on my map using lots of colored pins and pens to indicate different units and conventions. It can be quite a work of art by the end of the day.

There is no more fightable map than one that Jon Kluck puts his hands on. The goal is to have a board that someone familiar with the mission can walk up to with no explanation and "visualize the battle-field." Jon had that talent.

I stood tall at the edge of the ramp and gave Jon a look, and before I spoke, he said, "Don't worry about it, sir, I got it."

I responded, "You're in charge. See you in Baghdad."

CHAPTER 3

The War Machine Starts Turning

I BELIEVE MY JOURNEY TO IRAQ started the day I arrived at Fort Carson in Colorado and reported to duty with the 3rd Armored Cavalry Regiment (3rd ACR). That day was 11 September 2001.

I had just returned to the States from a one-year assignment in South Korea. While in Korea, I was a war planner. I was fresh out of the Armor Captain Career Course and was full of energy to plan, and plan I did. When I wasn't writing orders for operational missions, the planning staff would dust off and update war plans. For the first time in my career, I really felt like I was doing the real thing. Whether it was defending terrain below the demilitarized zone or attacking north into the strong North Korean defenses, I felt my work was relevant and important. My orders had to be concise, accurate, and creative. Any mistakes I made as a planner affected the individual soldiers.

Conventional tactics and planning procedures wouldn't work; creativity was the best weapon.

After a year of separation from my family, Kim and I spent several weeks taking it easy with family and friends. Like a sailor back from sea, I was able to amuse them with stories about my travels and adventures. It had been an incredible trip. Whether it was about sneaking onto a Chinese army installation for a rugby game or about riding elephants in the jungles of Thailand, I kept my audience entranced. But everyone knew that I was off to Fort Carson, my dream assignment. I had volunteered to serve a year in Korea to guarantee my spot there. I had even turned down two commands in Korea to wait for one at Carson. It was my mecca: skiing, hunting, fishing, hiking, camping, and, of course, the 3rd Armored Cavalry Regiment. 3rd U.S. CAV is the last heavy cavalry left in the Army. It is an honor to serve in the same unit as some of the most famous leaders in the history of our country: Patton, Polk, and Roosevelt, to name a few.

At 1000 hours, 11 September 2001, I was to report to the headquarters of 3rd Squadron to meet the squadron commander and receive my in-brief and job assignment. Kim and I decided to go to the gym early that day, so that I could get my workout in before starting my first day of work. Between sets my eyes caught the television. Although I knew it was tuned to the news, it looked like a trailer for an action movie was on the screen. It looked so real. I walked closer and saw that this was actually live, breaking news. I was stunned and asked one of the men walking underneath the televisions to turn up the sound. I remember hearing the words "terrorist plot," then saw the footage of the second plane making impact. My shock turned to anger.

I yelled over to Kim, "Get over here! We've been attacked."

Kim stumbled across the gym, so focused on the televisions that she kept running into machines. She said, "I don't understand."

I said, "Neither do I, but we are under attack." For the first time in my adult life, I didn't know what to do. Like the rest of America, I stood and stared at the television in disbelief. Then the newscast cut to the Pentagon. Then I knew what to do.

"Kim, get your stuff. We need to go. I need to get my gear. We're at war."

She knew what I meant, and she didn't hesitate. We ran to the truck and drove off the post to our friends' house, where we had been staying until we could move into our housing on post. I stayed only long enough to shower and grab my Army bags. I kissed Kim and held her tight. I wasn't sure if I was coming home again. After living in Korea, I had practiced this drill several times a month. But this time, it was, without any doubt, no drill. Looking into her eyes, I saw her pride overpowering her fear. She knew that duty was calling me. Neither of us knew what was next. We hadn't even moved in yet. All our stuff was in storage. Our cats were in the basement of our friends' house. There was so much left to do. We were in the middle of a national emergency, and there was no time to worry about the details.

I drove to work as fast as I could, but was stopped by the six-hour traffic jam of everyone trying to get back to headquarters. Every car had to be inspected. We were so unsure of what the next target was that the post commander had to close the gates and search every vehicle that was coming on post. Even the soldiers had to be inspected. I sat frustrated in my truck, waiting. Fortunately, as she always does, Kim had packed me a lunch. I spent that time listening to descriptions of people jumping from windows, heroic actions, and lots of people dead or dying. I was so confused, I couldn't even cry. I didn't know how to feel. I just wanted to get to work and find out what our orders were. I thought about my friends in New York City, and others at the Pentagon, and wondered where they were, and if they were still alive. It was all so confusing.

Finally on post, I made my way to the headquarters building and was told to stand by in the briefing room. I sat with the rest of the officers and waited for our boss to get his brief. After a few more hours of waiting, the boss came in. Even he looked confused—and angry.

"Men, our nation was attacked by terrorists. We currently have no orders to mobilize, but need to get prepared for it. Stand your units down. I need to know how many families are affected by this and get them on leave as soon as possible. Go home and spend time with your wives and kids. This is a day for prayer."

We all stood and saluted. That was how I met my first boss in the 3rd ACR.

■　■　■

We were finally issued our deployment order on Valentine's Day, 2003, sixteen months after 11 September. It was a Friday morning, and Kim and I were enjoying a day off from our regular weekend skiing routine. We had been expecting the call, but not on the day reserved for lovers. February 14 was supposed to be a day off, one of the cherished days off I was actually able to take over the last year. Up to that point, I had already been away from home six of the last eight months. We had just enjoyed the morning, and I was already in the garage packing my ski gear for the rest of the weekend. Kim came into the garage and handed me the phone and said, "I think it's work," giving me that look I am so accustomed to when I have promised her some time alone and the phone calls me to duty. Being told to drive in to pick something up was not unusual for a troop commander on the weekend, but it also implied some amount of work. I had the drill down and was out the door within minutes. I thought it was odd that all the captains in the neighborhood were headed to the headquarters building. We passed with waves and uncertain looks. Some, already returning, were smiling and flashing lights, yelling out the window, "We're going to the big show!"

Upon arriving at work, I signed for my copy of the memorandum for record, "Deployment of the Regiment of Mounted Riflemen," which was written by the seventieth colonel of the regiment himself. That was all I looked at before hurrying back home, knowing that I was about to be part of history, but also knowing that I owed the rest of the day to my wife. As I entered the door, she looked into my hand. "Wow. That was fast. What happened?" she asked. I responded, "We got our deployment orders . . . we're finally going." That's how I felt. Finally. It was a relief after months of training. I had spent every free moment studying Iraq maps, tactics, Arab culture, reading the Koran, and sizing up every one of my men for readiness and potential. I had been studying for this final exam for years and was finally going to have the chance to take it. I was going to war as a troop commander. I was so proud. But Kim's hug felt pitiful. She was already crying, and it was hard for me to be sensitive.

I tried to read my memorandum to Kim: "The 3rd U.S. Cavalry Regiment will deploy to Central Command's area of responsibility in a number of weeks. Our equipment will be shipped overseas in a couple of days. When we link up with our equipment, we will build combat power in theatre and complete preparations to conduct combat operations. The personal responsibility of every member of the Regiment and every attached soldier that deploys with the Brave Rifles will be enormous."

Realizing that I was now reading it to myself, I continued under my breath, until the final two paragraphs:

"Finally, we will all do our duty. Duty requires high and demanding standards in combat. That duty obliges us to put the mission ahead of everything else, even ahead of personal comfort and safety. That sacrifice is difficult and harsh. Duty in combat calls for levels of self-sacrifice and dedication that are just not present at any other time. But that concept of duty has characterized American Soldiers of the past and will guide us well into the future.

"May God bless us and protect the Regiment as we answer the Nation's call. Signed, David A. Teeples, 70th Colonel of the Regiment."

Although I should have knelt to pray for my own protection, I instead did the next most logical thing—I cracked open a beer. After savoring a few long draughts, I called my first sergeant and all my lieutenants to announce the word. "It's official," I started. "Call your chain of command and let them know that a two-hour recall is in place … we have our deployment orders and are headed to the CENTCOM AOR. Call me back when you have complete notification."

Last on the alert roster were my parents. My father was excited. My mother cried. I had planned on spending some time with my wife after finishing the roster. What a joke. The phone rang all day. I could barely hold her in my arms before there came a knock on the door or another ring on the phone. We gave up on being sweet and postponed romance until this day was done. I owed her a big one.

We had just watched the movie *We Were Soldiers*, in which the colonel's wife receives word that the men are deploying to Vietnam and says, "Ladies, get out your best dresses … the men are going to want to have a ball." Indeed, we were scheduled for our regimental ball that very night. We were originally not excited about having to go to a ball on this special night of Valentine's. But with orders in hand, there was a new excitement about dining, toasting, drinking, and dancing with my fellow warriors.

Kim was not as excited. It was a moment of sobriety for her, not just the awkwardness of having to attend a formal ball in her second trimester of pregnancy, but just an overall feeling of nervousness. She felt as if each day could be our last together.

We had decided to try to have a baby as soon as all the signals were pointing to an uncertain war in Iraq and our eventual deployment. "I want to have a baby so I have something left of you," Kim had told me. "Something living and breathing that is you."

The ball started with a bit of a shock. We were at the Antler Adam's Mark Hotel, and the commander had pulled out all the stops to decorate for the event. But when I tried to drop Kim off at the hotel doors, several police cars were blocking the entrance to the drive. So we parked on the street and hurried in. Once inside, I thought it seemed unusual that there were several hundred soldiers and their dates in the lobby and not at the bar. The buzz in the lobby was that there was a bomb in the underground parking lot attached to the building. We had dealt with antiwar rallies for the last six months, but this was going too far. Our event was a good target, with all the leadership of the entire regiment in one room in a single building. The colonel considered canceling the evening, but we all felt confident that it was just an antiwar protester making a statement. I am proud of the right to protest and will defend that freedom with my own life. But when someone breaks federal law and puts others in danger with a hoax, that privilege is revoked.

After an hour wait, hotel security confirmed that there was no bomb, and in typical Army style, it was not mentioned again. Before long, the queues for the cash bars were long and everyone was asked to take their seats. As the bugler called the crowd to attention, it was clear that the presentation of the colors were next. The short ceremony had special meaning tonight. Two thousand men and women stood at attention and watched as the color guard brought in the United States flag and the regimental guidon, both under armed guard by the detachment. At any formal dinner, the colors are presented to the highest-ranking officer, who gives the command to "post" the colors. It is a reminder that we are men in uniform and that we owe our respects to those who have provided our freedom. The regimental colors are a beautiful sight. Atop the flagpole are all the campaign streamers of the 3rd U.S. Cavalry history: three from the Mexican War, eight from the Indian Wars, three from the Civil War, one from Spain, one from the Philippine Insurrection, three from World War II, and two from the Gulf War. The bearer always seems to strain under the weight of the colors. Behind the U.S. flag follows the 3rd ACR.

During the National Anthem, men and women cried together, but all stood at the perfect position of attention. Before we stood at ease, there were the toasts.

"To the president of the United States . . . To the commander in chief!"

"To the United States Army . . . To the Army!"

"To III Corps . . . To the Phantom Corps!"

"To Fort Carson . . . To the Mountain Post!"

"To the Regiment of Mountain Riflemen, Brave Rifles . . . Veterans!"

"To the Troopers . . . To the Troopers!"

"To Our Fallen Comrades". . . (Silence, to honor the fallen)

"Gentlemen, please seat your ladies". . . (time to seat the ladies) "To the ladies!"

As I drank deeply to the last toast, I set down my glass and gave Kim a tender kiss. With all that had happened that day, it was finally time to give Kim some attention. It was not the perfect evening, but it was our life. She was able to hide her prior nervousness and now smiled with pride as I sat with my lieutenants and noncommissioned officers, and continued to toast until the dinner was served. These were the men I was off to fight with, and these were the women we were going to leave behind. Three of the four women at the table were pregnant, and the fourth would be married within the week. We were family—not just the table, but the entire room.

One of my favorite lieutenants asked with a shit-eating grin, "Sir, are you ready?"

He knew that if we weren't dressed up, I would have socked him once in the arm for asking such a dumb question.

I responded, "Well, if we aren't now, we'll just figure it out when we get there."

That answer was enough for him. But I knew he was nervous. He had only been here for two weeks, but was already prepared in his heart and mind. He was going to have to learn his job at war. He was ready to pick my brain right there at the table because he was so eager to learn.

I had to stop him and say, "L.T., this night is for us to relax and enjoy being part of the cavalry. We will not discuss war and tactics in front of the ladies. Bring your maps in on Monday and I'll fill your head . . . until then, pour yourself a whiskey and make polite conversation."

After some genuine laughter from the entire table, I added, "And, don't worry . . . we will be victorious!" We all tapped our glasses together at my new toast.

■ ■ ■

We spent our final weeks before deployment to Iraq thinking back to the lessons we had learned from our rotation at the Joint Readiness Training Center (JRTC) the previous October in Louisiana. JRTC is the Army's infantry branch proving grounds. Unlike the armor branch, infantry measures success by matter of inches on a map. It conducts missions in urban areas and clears buildings in a fashion that we rarely study. When we go to any other training center, we conduct contiguous battle planning and execution. We had moved across the Mojave Desert at the National Training Center (NTC), in Fort Irwin, California, and tried to fight like Patton or Rommel across forty kilometers of sand and dust to the objective. I had already had two tours at the NTC and was ready to learn something new in the "jungles" of JRTC. JRTC is located in Fort Polk, Louisiana, and replicates terrain that we never imagine fighting in as armor officers. But as a cavalry-man, it was my next test, and the road leading to it had been long.

In April 2002, I had spent the last six weeks at Pinion Canyon Maneuver Area, which is where the troops at Fort Carson train. It is like a mini-NTC in the southeast corner of Colorado, with nothing but sand, valleys, and big sky. One day, I got a frantic call from one of the captains in the training section, asking me to leave that night to go to Fort Drum, in upstate New York, and conduct coordination with 2nd Brigade, 10th Mountain Division, in regard to the JRTC rotation I was scheduled for that October. There was no thinking about it—my dreams were starting to come true.

I had to break into my house to unpack my field gear (I didn't have my keys) and repack some clean uniforms to take to Fort Drum. Kim got home from work just in time to turn around and drive me to Denver. I explained to her how important this mission was for me. 2nd Brigade, 10th Mountain Division, had just returned from Afghanistan after kicking Taliban ass, and was going to be able to teach me a tremendous amount about fighting terrorists. My expectations were high, and I was not let down. I had been selected to be the "heavy team" for the mission. The commander, Colonel Wilkerson, was ready for the fight at JRTC, eager to prove that the brigade was ready to go back to Afghanistan and give some more fight. When colonels go to these training centers, they are there to prove something. Colonel Wilkerson had just come back from Operation Enduring Freedom and was ready to teach the training center some new lessons of his own. He made that clear the first time I met him, and I was proud to be under such proven leadership.

I ended up spending most of the summer in both New York and Louisiana. I went to several conferences with the 10th Mountain Division and even attended a few field-training exercises. It was a shame that I couldn't bring my tanks, because it was hard to replicate for the infantry how powerful a force I was going to be at Fort Polk during JRTC. Some of the commanders gave me credit, but others wanted me to be sure that I was paying attention to how they fought.

Between my trips to New York, I returned to Fort Carson and took my soldiers out into the field to try to replicate scenarios I had observed. It was difficult. The only way to make your soldiers learn is to create realistic training. Most important, you have to make it fun. It is hard to make a tank crewman think in terms of meters instead of kilometers. It is also hard to make the mountains of Colorado look like the swamps of Louisiana. My men took the training seriously and saw my determination. There was rarely a time when I was not brainstorming new ideas with my lieutenants, whether it was on my white board with markers in my office or with sugar packets at the bar. I wanted to show up and fight with the same reputation that the 3rd ACR carries with it wherever it goes—not to mention the fact that I was being judged and taught by men who had just fought a real war.

As October approached and we completed our tank and Bradley gunnery, my men were ready to fight. We deployed our vehicles to JRTC and conducted a live fire exercise within the first few days. Unfortunately, we arrived the same time as a hurricane. Even in the endless rain, my men performed exceptionally. The live-fire range executed a canned scenario that allowed my tanks and Bradleys to use all their weapon system on "hard targets," minus our TOW missiles. I finally got to show my comrades the power I was bringing to the fight. My crew fired twenty main gun rounds with perfect accuracy, and I was able to pump over a thousand rounds of .50-caliber machine gun during the training. It is times like those that I think, "This is why I joined the Army." It was a blast.

The fun was just beginning as we refitted to go into the field for the three-week final exam. As I have four heavy maneuver platoons, it is easy for mission planners to place the combat power under the command of more senior officers. But rather than farming me out to each of the three maneuver battalions, Colonel Wilkerson decided to fight me in a configuration with my own men, as a troop, and gave me the same honors as his battalion commanders. This move showed his trust and confidence in me. He spoke to us the night before we went into the exercise and asked us to think of every casualty as real. He cried, thinking back to the men he had lost in Afghanistan, and made sure we knew how serious he was. I fully understood his order and made sure my leaders did as well. Ironically, most of our time was spent fighting through mines; my men became experts at breaching all types of minefields. In fact, for weeks, we fought with few training casualties and moved around the battlefield at will and with the power afforded to well-trained tank units.

The last week's training had the most lasting effect. JRTC has an entire city to train in, and even hires civilians to "live" in it and sometimes act as hostages. One night I drove my tank into a giant hole and flipped it on its side. I nearly killed myself, but didn't miss any of the fight. I stood on the side of the tank until it was righted, continuing to issue orders on my radios. Although it was an infantry fight, the lessons my men learned in the "city" had direct influence on their successes in Iraq.

We needed to study the urban fight the most. We were more than capable at fighting an enemy lined up or maneuvering, but fighting terrorists in the streets was a task that we seldom thought we'd confront. I had studied it for months, but couldn't believe what I saw at Fort Polk. It exemplified incredible bravery and teamwork. Being part of it at JRTC was our first eye-opener.

Back at Carson, a few weeks before deploying, I was sitting around talking with my senior noncommissioned officers about all the training we had done, asking for ideas about anything we might have missed. Sergeant First Class McNichols, whom I will always consider a dear friend, said, "You dumb-ass tankers are eventually going to have to get off your tanks and fight in the streets. Sir, why don't we spend a few days practicing arrests and clearing houses? You guys could even use some work on dismounted patrols. I've seen you out there practicing and you look like shit!"

Although Sergeant First Class McNichols had been in Panama and was an instructor at several elite infantry schools, we spent the next hour talking trash back to him about his personal opinions and made it clear that tankers "don't get off the boat" (from *Apocalypse Now*) for anything. I responded, "Mac, that is why we have infantry attached . . . we don't walk." How wrong I was.

CHAPTER 4

My Life as a Texan

I WAS ADOPTED AT BIRTH. I rarely think about this fact. But when I think about going to war and making a name for myself as a warrior, I think about mythological heroes.

In many tales throughout mythology, there is often something unusual about a hero's birth and upbringing. In the oldest hero myth, *Gilgamesh*, featuring the Mesopotamian hero of the Tigris-Euphrates region and who is the standard for all heroes, Gilgamesh was born two-thirds god (son of a bull, Uruk) and one-third man. Romulus and Remus, the founders of Rome, were left to suckle on a she-wolf after Amulius, who did not want any potential heirs, abandoned them. Like me, many gods and mortals in Greek mythology did not know their birth fathers or parents at all. Each hero overcame his difficult beginnings to lead men and win battles. I have always kept that in the back of my mind. It makes me feel that I automatically have a leg up on others—I was born in the mold of a leader.

My parents, Judy and John Rozelle, told me when I was young that they were told my birth parents might have had some American Indian ancestry. The knowledge that I may have Native American blood flowing through my veins gives me a deeper love for my country.

I was blessed with the most incredible parents a child could ever ask for. I am often asked what the differences were growing up as an adopted child. For my sister, Amy, and I, there are none. John and Judy are my parents, as much as any birth parent would be. I am more like my father than I will ever admit, just as he was like his father. My wife would describe me more as a hybrid between my father and his brother Dean. When you boil it down, I am my father's son; I laugh like my father, enjoy the same books, and most of the same music.

Dad and I even have the same preference in women. Kim and my mother have a lot in common. Both are Carolina girls with Carolina educations, who know and love Southern traditions, and both are similar in height, build, and temper. I think their biggest similarity is that they are both dreamers; not only can they see something good in everything that happens, but they always have glorious plans for the future. That is what I love.

My father ensured that I had both everything he had or couldn't have. He wanted to be sure that from my first days of school that I had every opportunity to get ahead. As a child, we traveled Europe, and I became comfortable in foreign places. He would always talk to me about the sea, and what it was like exploring the world. He wanted to raise me as a Renaissance man (artist, poet, lover, and warrior) and release me to explore the world unafraid. Although he never missed any of my sporting events, he also ensured that I wasn't falling behind on my studies of Latin and Greek. Even when times were tough for us financially, he found ways for me to continue to attend private schools and educational summer camps. When it came time to go off to college, he took a week off from work and drove me to all the schools he hoped I would go: Harvard, Princeton, Georgetown, UVA, Duke, and Davidson. You should have seen the pleasure on his face when I told him that I was sold on Davidson and wanted to apply early.

Inscribed on the bell in the tower of the main administration building at Davidson is:

In memory of our soldier dead,
To you from falling hands
We throw the torch;
Be yours to hold it high.

I saw that as a sign that Davidson was the school for me.

My dad was a homebuilder. He is the hardest-working man I have ever known, a seven-day-week man. My mother was an early childhood educator, and gets complete credit for any of my academic successes. Actually, she continues to take credit for instructing me on most things at which I am successful. She deserves plenty of that credit, as she spent the prime of her life driving me and my sister around Austin, Texas, to piano lessons, soccer practice, and theatre class. She did all that in addition to her full-time job as a teacher. I guess that explains why she is having such a hard time retiring from education now. She needs that drive in her life. She walks six miles a day, like a soldier, in any weather and at 0600 hours, sharp.

She can be emotional, but she's strong. On 3 July 2003, Mom was the first to peek her head into my room at Walter Reed Army Medical Center in Washington, D.C., where the Army had shipped me to recover from my injury. She came in with a forced smile, showing her strength, as she always does in a crisis. But as soon as our eyes met, she broke into tears. I was again her little boy, unable to move and looking and feeling sick. She practically dove into the bed with me and almost pulled out my IV. I was home, and she was there for me. I could tell that she had been practicing her first words to me the entire way up from South Carolina.

"David, remember when you ran that race at Zilker Park in Austin? Remember how sick I was after a bad batch of enchiladas the night before, but I took you to your race anyway? Do you remember how you started to fall behind and I started running beside you, encouraging you to go faster?" she started between tears, and grabbed my hand.

"Do you remember me running the rest of that race with you? I did, and we finished together." Looking into my eyes, she said, "I am here again, by your side. We are going to do this together!"

What more can I say about my mother? She is my best friend and toughest critic. And she is the daughter of Colonel (Retired) Lehman Maybe "Frosty" Bauknight. Papa Frosty, as I called him, was, and is, one of the most influential men in my life.

■   ■   ■

Papa Frosty was the son of a farmer in Pickens County, South Carolina, one of five children. As a child, he survived polio, but was scarred and had stunted growth in his right leg. He always walked with a limp. He was not the first to go to college, as his family was quite proud of their academic achievements, and chose to attend Clemson Agriculture and Machinery, now known as Clemson University. He received a B.S. in Forest Resource Management in June of 1937. He was commissioned through the Clemson Reserve Officer Training Corps and served as a second lieutenant in the United States Army Reserve.

Although his heart had initially been in teaching, there was a two-front war going on and he wanted to contribute. Ignoring the pleas of his family, as they worried about his leg, he started looking for a way to volunteer. I will never be able to tell the story as my grandfather did those many mornings fishing on the pier at Pawley's Island, South Carolina, but I will try.

"Now, David, the country was at war. It was the Big One, WWII. Most of the men had already been drafted and things seemed desperate. Do you know when the war was?" Papa Frosty was always the teacher.

When questioned like this, I usually acted really interested in the depth of my bait, or the tension in my line.

So, after a short class on World War II, and in hopes that I might remember it next time, he said, "Pay attention, David, because history repeats itself, and you may be called to defend this great country of ours. It was 1940 when I finally activated and went to support the war at the Pentagon in the District of Columbia."

Seeing where my eyes had immediately gone, he pulled up his pants leg and laughed, "You should have seen those doctors the day that they saw my legs. Back then, we didn't wear shorts like you young 'uns do all the time, so the first time anyone saw my leg was at my physical. I wore my pants in to undress behind the curtain, but had them off when the doctors came in to examine me. You should have seen their faces."

Papa Frosty stopped to slap his knee and chuckle. He had the most soothing laugh, and would usually end each episode of laughter by saying something like, "Well now, business is picking up!"

Serious again, he said, "Now, those boys didn't want me to go and fight. I told them that I didn't have to fight, I just wanted to help, and there had to be something for a man with one leg shorter than the other to do to help our boys overseas. They found something for me to do, all right, and assigned me as an adjutant general."

The spirit in Papa Frosty inspired the same emotion in me after my injury. He spent September 1940 to October 1945 on active duty, mostly at the Pentagon. During his tour, he served several times as an aide de camp and assisted as an intelligence analyst. He returned to the reserves and retired as a colonel in 1959.

After the war, he returned to teaching and to farming trees. He was a professor of agricultural economics at Clemson University from 1947 until he retired in 1983. He hardly retired though, as he traveled the South lecturing, consulting, and speaking on agriculture. His trees also kept him busy, even if he was just walking through the woods enjoying some blackberries.

Papa Frosty died in 1991. He was a leader, and touched the hearts and minds of thousands of students and faculty alike.

■   ■   ■

Dad is quick to remind me that the Rozelle family also has a meritorious service record throughout the history of our country. As I said before, we are Texans—my ancestors moved there in the early 1800s. Texans have a hard time walking away from a fight.

My father was named after another warrior, John Rozelle. John was one of his great uncles and a celebrated man in the Rozelle family. He was born in 1897 in Alto, Texas. He served with the United States Expeditionary Forces in France from 1918 to 1919. Although he survived the fierce fighting in the trenches of World War I, he died in 1929 due to complications from a German gas attack.

John Rozelle's military portrait hangs in my grandmother's house. Since I was a child, I've thought about what it must have been like to fight that war. In the picture, he looks handsome and severe, but with rosy cheeks and a slight smile. He must have been a hell of a man.

My father's first cousin "Buck" Whitt attended Texas A&M University from 1949 to 1952 and was commissioned a year early, in order to attend pilot training. At the time, U.S. forces desperately needed pilots to assist efforts in Korea.

Buck never made it to Korea. He was killed in a crash during the last two weeks of advanced training in F-86D fighter aircraft at Nellis Air Force Base, Nevada. He was scheduled to depart for Korea immediately following this training. Buck was the golden child in the family, and many hopes crashed with him that day.

Ten years later, in August 1963, Dad graduated from the University of North Texas. With the memory of Buck still so fresh, there was some concern in the family when Dad entered the Air Force Officers' Training School in September. He was commissioned as a second lieutenant on 20 December 1963, and graduated navigator training school on 15 December 1964. His primary assignment was to the 432nd Military Airlift Wing, Charleston Air Force Base, South Carolina. He spent from January 1965 to September 1968 on flight duty in support of U.S. forces worldwide, with a focus of flights into Southeast Asia, Europe, and South America.

Dad made me understand the importance of men serving their country. From an early age, as we traveled Europe, I learned from him how unique we are as Americans to have an all-volunteer Army. He believes that military service is a right of passage for Americans. If you cannot serve your country in any other way, then you owe it to your country to defend her for a tour of duty.

Whenever I would talk about all the great freedoms in America, he would often look at me and say, "David, freedom isn't free."

■   ■   ■

Dad's little brother, Dean, is almost equal with my father in his influence and participation in my upbringing. Dean has been at every major event in my life, from my coming home from the hospital at birth to my second time coming home from the hospital, from war. He is a friend, companion, hunting buddy, dive buddy, drinking buddy, counselor, and confidant.

Dean has no military background, as he was too young for the early part of Vietnam and had a low draft number on the far end. But Dean is a history buff and military enthusiast, so you would never know that he isn't former military. Most important, Dean taught me how to shoot, hunt, and move with a rifle through the woods. I was with Dean the first time I killed a dove, quail, rabbit, and deer.

Dean and I would go hunting on weekends from the time I was twelve years old, and he painstakingly taught me how to shoot. He taught me the traditional way, on a rest, for years before allowing me to move into standing positions. Before I could plink at cans, like most of my friends were already doing, he was taking me through the steps on target paper. The first few times with a rifle, I didn't even get ammunition. We just worked on holding steady, breathing, and trigger pull. By the time I was fourteen, I was finally allowed to shoot a pistol, but we had to start all over again. Standing drills, with new breathing lessons. It was the same pull, but with much more anticipation. Dean treats shooting like ballet. It must be smooth, rhythmic, and easy.

As Dean studied the future war in Iraq, he believed we would be fighting more as policemen, and started loading me up with police manuals and techniques. He also gave me some studies on justifiable police shootings, in order to make me more aware of justification of violent force in a police environment. He wanted to be sure that I was ready.

I learned to shoot with Dean, and knowing how to shoot a pistol saved my life in Iraq.

■ ■ ■

Growing up in Austin, Texas, I always knew that Texans were a different breed, but it wasn't until I grew up that I realized what being a Texan meant. As a young student, it did not seem unusual to me that the Texas history book was larger than the U.S. history books. Texas is bigger. In that class we learned about explorers, frontiersmen, and war-riors. Those were the men and women that came to and created Texas. Wherever you go, you see the state flag flying; the colors represent bravery, purity, and loyalty. We celebrate our independence day every year with the same pride as the Fourth of July. People who don't understand Texans are those who don't know about or feel pride in where they came from. I am a sixth-generation Texan and will always be proud of that heritage.

It should be no surprise to anyone that we consider ourselves from another country entirely. The fact is no less true than when you find a Texan out of Texas. As if living out some prophecy, we don our biggest hats, pull on our highest-heeled boots, and hit the town, warm-ing up our throats to yell loudly, ready to two-step at a moment's notice. And that is how I left Texas, headed for college in North Car-olina. The question wasn't, "Am I ready for Carolina?" but "Is Carolina ready for me?"

I showed up at Davidson College in Davidson, North Carolina, on 19 August 1991. I arrived to an empty campus and reported to Davidson's football summer camp. It was only a three-week camp, but it was a great introduction to Davidson. The camp itself was a bless-ing; imagine showing up to a new college and within the first day hav-ing fifty new friends.

I didn't go to Davidson to become a football star, but I loved the game. It is a game about teamwork, strength, and strategy. I was fully committed to the team until school started and I started learning about some other great activities, like being a freshman in college. Before the end of the season, high school sports injuries (dislocated shoulders, broken collarbones) started catching up with me. My shoulders were weak and I couldn't enjoy the game any more. My grades were suffering, and I couldn't do it all. Spring semester, 1992, I decided to focus on my studies. Well, actually, I was pledging a fraternity. College turned out to be everything I had expected and wanted it to be. Mostly, it was total freedom and lots of fun with new friends.

I was immediately defined as a Texan, a football player, and a frat boy, but it was the Army that prepared me for life. All year, I had laughed at my best friend, Patrick Malcor, as he dressed up in his nerdy ROTC uniform and went to class. Each day I saw him in it, I couldn't help but laugh, as he looked like an out-of-place Boy Scout. He even had to miss a few parties because of his monthly training commitment. But after a year of suffering through three different jobs, a full course load, and my fraternity duties, I realized that he was the one laughing at me. Patrick was on a full scholarship to Davidson, and got a check each month for going into the woods one day a week and one weekend a month to play war. Patrick talked me into going to one of their "labs," where we crawled through the mud and ran an obstacle course with rubber weapons. I loved it. Three months out from the end of my freshman year, I found myself in the ROTC office signing up to go the Airborne School at Fort Benning, Georgia, to jump out of airplanes, as a recruiting assignment to see if I would enjoy the Army.

With Patrick as my training partner and guide, I spent the last two months of school getting in shape to go airborne. Recruiting weeks are famous for having stiff physical requirements, and for sending people home the first week if they can't meet the physical standards. You spend three weeks preparing yourself to jump out of an airplane five times. It was my first glimpse at part of the real Army, with real soldiers. I found all the physical training demanding and rewarding. We walked two miles to the site of our physical training in the morning and then two miles home to change. After thirty minutes of cleaning our quarters and ourselves, we walked two miles back to chow, and then started training. I had never slept as well for so short a period.

After three weeks of training side by side, Patrick and I finally made our first jump. It was clear to me as I took that first step into the sky that the Army life was the life for me. My father was there at graduation to pin on my coveted airborne wings, which is a lifetime parachutist badge worn on all military uniforms.

Back at school, I was eager to sign up and start getting my check, but I wasn't eligible to be awarded a scholarship. Turned out that my freedom of freshman year was already impacting my life. I was told to buckle down on my grades, take ROTC as an elective, and plan to attend ROTC basic camp the next summer. I did all those things and excelled.

When I headed off to Fort Knox, Kentucky, I brought with me to camp a full year of military experience and airborne wings. Basic camp is a basic training environment with a leadership potential focus. You do the standard six-week basic training, with drill sergeants and the standard training lesson, but with attached ROTC evaluators to evaluate the cadets. Again, I found the training challenging but rewarding. I was learning skills that I still use today, and I paid attention. I won one of two scholarships available for my training battalion, and was an honor graduate for my rotation.

The lessons I learned springboarded me into ROTC and I found myself teaching and leading after only my first full year. After our advanced course at Fort Bragg, North Carolina, another six-week program dedicated to leadership development, I was again an honor graduate. My excellence in the early military arts can be attributed to my casual leadership style. From the beginning, I treated leadership positions no different than I had as team captain for soccer or football. Being a team captain means no special privilege, but gives you the responsibility to make decisions with the referees for the team. As a team captain, I learned that teams can win only when they pull together, and that the captain is responsible for bringing them together. A dedicated team working together will always win. I took those early lessons with me to develop a leadership style as a cadet, and I was successful. All I had to do now was stay out of trouble, pass my classes, and I was on the road to a military career. I was commissioned a second lieutenant in May 1995, and pinned by my mother and father.

At Davidson, I studied and received a degree in English literature, with an emphasis in late nineteenth and early twentieth century English and American naturalists. I focused my studies on poetry. Maybe my love of poetry led me into the Army, with its romantic appeal of traveling around the world. I can't tell you what I would have done had it not been for the Army, except maybe become a professional student. I have to admit, I was an odd addition to weekly poetry readings and working sessions, but my poetry was pure and from the heart.

There was one event that completed my college experience. Before graduating from Davidson, I wrote the Army a letter and explained that I had never had the chance to study abroad. I wanted to see and experience parts of Europe that I thought I might not get a chance to see before I got locked into my military career. I requested a delayed entry after my commissioning to spend six months traveling on my own. To my surprise, the request was granted.

I started my trip that May, the day after graduation. After a few months exploring our national parks out West, I traveled Europe from England to Turkey, mostly following the Mediterranean coast. I had many adventures along the way through France, Spain, Gibraltar, the Costa del Sol, Italy, and then Greece. But I fell in love with Turkey. It was my first time in Southwest Asia, and I was more comfortable there than any other place, even more than Europe. I spent a month in Turkey, and two weeks of that in a place called Olympia, where I slept in a tree house and paid only for my meals, which averaged about five dollars a day. I spent my days talking to travelers, swimming in the ocean, and thinking about life. It prepared me for the journeys ahead.

■   ■   ■

I came back to the States in October. My next big trip abroad, to the Middle East, would not come until much later, after several years of military training and jobs. I was trained as an armored crewman and tank platoon leader at Fort Knox, Kentucky, at the Armor Officer Basic Course. I served all the appropriate positions in 3/66 Armored Battalion, 1st Brigade, Fort Hood, Texas: tank platoon leader, mortar platoon leader, and as an executive officer for a tank company. It was great being home, just an hour from Austin.

I would be lying if I didn't mention that Austin was a bit of a distraction. Back home, after five years away, with a good job in the Army and having just traveled Europe, I had some stories to tell. Fort Hood was a great introduction to the Army. We were a test unit, testing navigation and communication equipment on M1A1 Abrams main battle tanks. I was able to participate in two separate rotations at the National Training Center in Fort Irwin, California. I also earned my expert infantry badge (EIB), as I was responsible for the mortars in both 3/66 Armored Battalion and 1/22 Infantry Battalion, during a period where I split my platoon and trained up two separate platoons for each battalion. Although I had some incredible experiences as a leader at Fort Hood, earning my EIB was the first time my men were really proud of me, and that felt good. It is still one of my highest honors.

After three and a half years, I knew the platoon leader positions well, but had not spent any time as a junior staff officer. I had just gotten married and was months away from becoming a captain. I volunteered to go to Kuwait with 1/10 Cavalry Squadron, as part of Operation Desert Spring. I was assigned as the Brigade Forward Logistics Officer (S4). It was my first time back in the region since my time in Turkey, under quite different circumstances. Stepping off the plane and trying to breathe in the super-heated air was an easy reminder that I was a thousand miles south of my last visit. It was August 1999, and it was 135 degrees. I wasn't sure if it could get hotter than Texas in the summer. Boy, did I have a lot to learn.

After taking a few days to get used to the heat, we got to work. As the S4, I was assigned a vehicle and a cell phone. My first phone only lasted a day, as I left it on the dash and it melted while I ran some paperwork into a building on Camp Doha, Kuwait. After a few weeks, I got into acquisitioning supplies from the local economy. I spent my days driving the crazy streets of Kuwait, finding local merchants and buying everything from basketballs to plastic pipe for the guys out in the field. My experiences were another window into the Arab people. I bought a translation of the Koran and tried to understand the people better. Although the Koran was a good way to understand some things, I had to go out and get a book on Arab history and culture to clear things up a little. I learned a lot in those six months.

LETTER HOME, 23 AUGUST 1999:

Howdy Folks,

Things are finally starting to settle down into a normal schedule, and I have had some time to reflect on my existence here. Must admit that I miss home, and everything that home implies. I went for a run this morning, as I have been trying to make a regular schedule for myself. Trying to beat the heat, I got up about 0430 and headed out to stretch. The winds had shifted over the night and sent air inland that was about 80% humidity and 110 degrees F. By the end of the run, I literally looked as if someone had soaked me with a water hose. Hopefully, the winds will shift back within a few days. The dry heat is not too bad, once you get over the initial shock. I am having a hard time imagining how people lived through the recorded highs earlier in the summer of temperatures in the 140s, when we have people in the U.S. checking out when thermometers are barely breaking 100F. We have been lucky, so far there are no heat casualties. Last rotation a guy had a heart attack while suffering from heatstroke. I have already once in my life held the hand of a soldier suffering from heatstroke and convulsions, which is a terrifying moment. I got my guys a truckload of bikes to get around the small post here, which beats the hell out of walking. We make a motley bunch, but the guys are much quicker running errands and happy too.

I have made several trips to Kuwait City, and, so far, am impressed. I have scheduled a tour of the city through the morale office here on post. I am the most interested in getting off post to tour. The guys just want to go sit in some refrigerated pool. They must go though, in order for me to justify the trips. I figured that I would send some initial impressions to you. Despite my month sojourn throughout Turkey, I am still becoming accustomed to Arab culture and architecture. The first things you notice while driving around are the beautiful doors and entryways on the homes; be it a palace or a shack. When someone does something great, rather than receiving the keys to the city, you receive the doors to the city. Like the Greek and Roman use of the façade, the doorway represents the owner's wealth and religious devotion. Doorways are very important, and are represented with incredible woodwork and design, and usually contain a prayer. I am quickly reminded of my father's doors and entryways into his homes he built at Wren Valley; true masterpieces.

The wealthy live downtown and have houses right along the major roads. The poor and the servants live in ghettos on the outskirts of the city, or in squatter settlements at the edge of the camel ranches. The second thing you notice about the home is the water containers on the ceiling. Even the palaces and mansions have visible water containers that look like insecticide containers on farm equipment. The country has plumbing in most buildings, but the water tank atop the homes is filled daily, and septic tanks are sucked daily. In urban areas, poor drainage leaves most street corners flooded with stagnant water.

One of my official duties is to conduct all airport runs for the unit. My first visit to the airport was quite nice. I am frequently required to make trips to the airport, as part of protocol and Red Cross missions. While trying to get in the VIP lounge, I befriended a police captain who dressed like a sheik. I am not sure what class he held, but he demanded respect from every Arab in the room. His first words spoken were, 'I don't take shit from any-body,' in near-perfect English. Thinking he had me off guard, I responded, 'Of course . . . except for me.' His chuckle was acknowl-edgment that I was alright and I immediately found myself on a silk-covered couch eating *shwarma* and falafel, and watching MTV Europe.

I made a visit to the U.S. Embassy. If I have a choice of assign-ment in the Middle East, it will certainly be the embassy in Kuwait. I was not allowed to even bring my camera inside, but hope to get some pictures during my promotion to captain cere-mony, which I am going to request at the embassy. The embassy was built in 1991 by one of the better builders in Kuwait, in a joint effort with Army Corps of Engineers. The stucco walls alternate with tiled murals, creating a blue/brown contrast that can only be compared to the eastern skies just after sunset in the desert. The inside is filled with beautiful rugs and paintings. It is truly the most beautiful fort I have ever seen. The dignitaries live in small "palaces" on the economy at the government's expense. Kuwait is safe enough now that those serving short tours are now allowed to have dependants accompany them for their tour. I am currently not living in a palace, but plan on visiting one next week. I will send a full report soon.

Divid (Indian pronunciation, which I often hear in Kuwait)

P.S. If you have looked for my location on a good map, I am at the tip of the northernmost peninsula that juts out into the Persian Gulf immediately north of Kuwait City, but south of Jahra and its southern bay.

LETTER HOME, 2 SEPTEMBER 1999:

Howdy Friends,

I am well and have few complaints beyond missing my wife and the comforts of home. I am continuing to adjust to the heat, although there are certainly days when I can't help but complain. They say that it will cool down to the lower hundreds and lows in the 90s by the end of the month. Apparently, these new temperatures will feel cool to our now adjusted bodies. I am not quite sure, but will let you know. Although my job is beginning to settle into a routine, each day can really vary in degree of work and pain. Days like today are nice. Frantic in the morning, but nothing to do but read and write in the afternoon.

The big trip this week was supposed to have taken me to the major attractions of Kuwait City, but we only made a few of them. We headed out early in my Suburban to the Al Qurain

Eternal Epic. According to the Kuwait POW Museum, during the occupation, it was a custom of the Iraqis to seize homes, rape the women, murder the men, and steal or destroy anything of reasonable value. This practice was more common in the beginning of '91, prior to the impending allied invasion. On 24 Feb 91, a group of nineteen civilian men took a stand against the occupying army, placing their lives in the hands of Allah. When the troops came to their home the civilians opened fire, and took positions around the two-house complex to defend them. The Iraqi army responded with tanks, mortars, and infantry soldiers. Although their stand-off lasted into the night, there was little of the house left when the Iraqis stormed the home. Only four men died in the battle, although numerous Iraqi soldiers died. Eight were taken prisoner, just to be taken into the street to be executed. Seven men hid in compartments around the home, and survived due to the aid of a power outage in the city. After the war, the emir visited the sight, and immediately declared it a monument to the fallen martyrs, and as criminal evidence of the Iraqi invasion. I have never experienced anything as graphic and terrifying as this monument. Like the Alamo, it represents the price of freedom that all men should be willing to take in defense of their country. Unlike the now cleaned Alamo and concentration camps, this museum is full of blood stains, dried guts, and rubble.

As if that visit wasn't sad enough, we then visited the Kuwaiti National POW and MIA museum. There are over 600 missing men, women, and children. There are still men and women being sought in Iraqi prisons by the International Red Cross. These are not soldiers, merely casualties of a frustrating and confusing occupation. I looked through an album of photographs of tortured and desecrated Kuwaitis. Seeing these disfigured shapes makes it hard for me to imagine that Iraq has never admitted to committing war crimes. Those days were certainly evil.

Here is where the trip ended, due to my Suburban losing its serpentine belt. I will spare you the details of being stranded on a desert highway in the Middle East. I am just glad I had food and water.

Until next time,

David

LETTER HOME, 18 SEPTEMBER 1999:

Hello Friends,

Things were really beginning to get in a rut here, and it is amazing how one night of fun and adventure can make up for several weeks of boredom. Actually, I have taken the opportunity to do some self-improvement: lifting weights, reading books, and thinking. Thinking and meditating on things is my most common way of passing time. I have had lots of opportunity to reflect on things important to me. I have also had time to think about things that aren't, and have started making an attempt to improve some things about myself. Self-reflection may be one of the most difficult tasks a man can do. I am happy with my success. The day-to-day schedule can really slow things down, especially in Kuwait.

At dinner a few nights ago, some permanent party officers (guys who are assigned here for the year) invited me for a trip downtown. Truly, these trips are the greatest and only big nights out to be had. We started out on Thursday afternoon, which is the Arabic Saturday in the workweek. We drove down the coast just as fishing boats were coming in to shore, with clouds of sea birds hovering around them. Children stood on the shore as if the boats were delivering candy, and were armed with bread and laughter. We weaved through traffic, as usual, and made our way beyond the ports to the heart of the city. We chose the coolest day of the summer, which was actually one of the first without sweltering heat. Although it was still around 108 deg, the temperature dropped into the 90s with a warm southern breeze. The cool evening allowed for a more comfortable trip as we snaked through the Arabic crowd outside the market. We went to the "Old *Souk*," which is the original marketplace for the city. The *souk* covers about eight or more city blocks, with a series of twisting streets and alleys. The market was largely open air, and most storefronts had merchandise spilling out into the streets. Each store was only about ten by ten feet, and usually only carried one type of merchandise. The *souk* can be compared to the Grand Bazaar of Turkey, but is intended more for the average Arab, rather than a tourist trade. You can buy anything from mangos to power saws and camel-keeping products. We chose the usual shopping day for Arabs, and as the weather had changed to pleasant, it was very crowded but orderly. There seemed to be no security, even at the gold shops, but everyone seems to be watching everything.

We were in the minority, but were certainly noticed as advertisers shouted unknown prices to us from competing stores as we entered others. Each street or alley sells like products, and store managers rarely carry more than one item. For instance, on one street you find only suitcases and handbags, but turn the corner and you find only spices and grain. Every price is negotiated. We were there primarily for gold, as I wanted to price what I had heard were remarkable deals. The gold *souks* take up several blocks, and overwhelm you with glitter and shimmer. The main area of the gold *souk* houses a department store, about the size of a Wal-Mart, that sells nothing but gold and jewels. The department store houses the finer stores, but is worth a walk-through—you can see all the sheiks and their veiled harems in tow. Rather than a department store, it seemed a living museum of wealth. I was impressed with the merchandise—some jewels were the size of baseballs—but I was poor. I spent most of my time in the neighborhood stores where the prices seemed more reasonable for similar products, just less presentation. You must haggle on prices, but seem only to be reducing the prices to the point where you are not getting ripped off. Gold is still gold, and is sold off of the gold standard. What you negotiate is the price of labor. Although haggling was fun, the prices still seemed astronomical for my first visit. I did find a group of back alley stores where third-country nationals made jewelry right in front of you. Their prices seemed affordable, but the work was a little cruder than the stores along the streets.

After exhausting ourselves with arguing over prices, we headed back to the open air kitchens to find something to eat. Along the way, we passed through the heart of the *souk*. Although I am used to open markets, I am always surprised by the modern practices of the Arab people. I saw fish that I had never seen before, that didn't even look edible. When you select meat, you select it off a hanging carcass, and can even cut it yourself. Chickens, ducks, and other fowl are selected alive and killed before your eyes to ensure freshness. We made our way to the bakery, where we selected a bag of goodies to eat with our *shwarmas*. We sat at a table and piled out our baked goods, while we waited on the *shwarmas* to be fixed. We had lots of falafel, curry meat pastry, goat cheese pastry, and a fried veggie ball that we named 'the moose turd,' due to its size, look, and consistency. All of the above were delicious. The chicken *shwarma* was shaved from the spit and quick fried with onions, tomatoes, and cilantro, then served on fresh pita bread. The lamb is served in the same manner, but with an added paste of *tomb*, which is a garlic-cheese mixture. The lamb was obviously my favorite.

We sat just under a mosque in a large open courtyard, and stuffed ourselves in true Arab style. Washing it all down with Pepsi, a local favorite, we all longed for and discussed beer. Just as the mosque tower began to drown all sound with the calls for prayer, with the breaks drowned by soothing wind, as if a sigh, I had a true epiphany. The moon was just rising over the gulf, and

children were setting off fireworks in the shadow of the Liberation Tower as the clerics called out for the hour of prayer from
the minarets. Our table sat in silence for a few moments, noticing everything at once. For that moment, as I watched the children play in the playground, I forgot about the passing cars and
the business of the market, and was soothed by the romance of
Kuwait.

Truly, before this point I had wondered how people for so
many generations had toughed it out in this God-forsaken place.
It was that moment that I will never forget, that I found the mys-
tique of this place. My meditation was interrupted, as if the call
for prayer was actually a call for smoke. We paid our debts, which
came to about one dinar (or $3 a person), and fought our way
back into the heart of the market.

Here, set aside by wooden fences and an open roof, was a well-
lit smoking lounge. As we entered, our servant was Mr. Ali, who
was presumably Pakistani. We took off our shoes and sat on well-
cushioned wooden benches, previously occupied by cats. The
place was full of men, as it is men-only, and could be a museum
of woodwork. We each were set up with water pipes and a hard-
ened apple-flavored tobacco that was then fired by burning coals.
As we puffed the pipes to fill the chamber with smoke, Mr. Ali
served us a constant supply of cinnamon and apple-flavored teas.
Relaxing on the cushions, we smoked and talked for several
hours, allowing conversation to turn to home and lots of brag-
ging. We finished our pipes and were served coffee. It was a coffee I have never had before. If Turkish coffee were unleaded, this

would certainly be diesel. A coffee that would turn my parents vampiric in its heroin-like caffeine effect. We settled with Mr. Ali for about a half a dinar apiece, about $1.50, for his services and made our way back into the now closing markets.

As the markets close, there is little to do, se we headed back towards post. Along the way we stopped at a café famous for its smoothies. Pleased with our patronage, the owner brought out a tray of pickled veggies and some delicious olives. Munching on these delights and fresh pita, we waited for our fresh smoothies. The smoothies were delicious and were a real treat to finish off the night. The wind was picking up, which caused blowing sand, a signal to retreat when hanging out in the desert. I look forward to my next trip on the town.

Next time,

David

After this entry, I had three more months to serve in Kuwait before returning home, which maintained in me a fascination and love affair with the Middle East long after my rotation ended. It is an affair that continues today.

Kim and I reuniting at the airport. Kim had our baby within days of this photograph being taken. She wiped away tears and looked beautiful. I was over thirty pounds lighter and unrecognizable to some. After all I had been through, I finally had a hero's welcome.

It was great to be home. My stump was hurting after my long day of travel, so I raised my leg for the picture. I could hardly stand up and Kim was about to burst. This was the first photo sent out to many friends, who then thought I had lost my leg up to the knee.

U.S. forces working side by side with the newly formed Hit police force. I'm in the middle (with the sunglasses), negotiating the release of a prisoner in return for some information. This photograph was taken just days before my injury.

The damaged Humvee towed back to camp. The blast had taken out the front end. My feet had been in the dark spot in front of the seat.

WHITE HOUSE PHOTO/SUSAN STERNER

It was an honor to greet the president so soon after returning home. Forrest, in the yellow blanket in the corner of the picture, met the president at only five days old.

JOEL BERMAN

After our tour of Air Force One. We placed Forrest in the president's chair. It was too bad we couldn't get a picture of that—I wanted to give him something to aspire to.

Proving that a missing limb was not going to slow me down, Kim and I snowshoed out to cut down our Christmas tree in Steamboat, Colorado. Forrest was waving at the camera from atop Kim's pack.

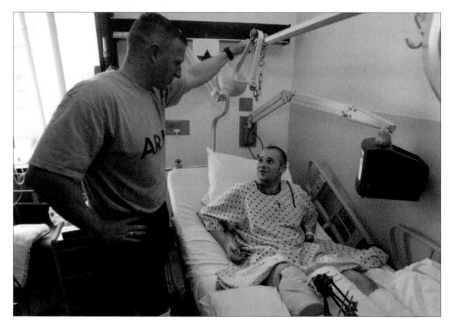

My favorite visits to Walter Reed were those when I was able to help a friend. Captain Marc Giammatteo is a Brave Rifles soldier who was injured about six months after I was. He has kept his leg and is recovering well at home. He is a hero.

The Rozelle family on a spring ski day in Arapaho Basin, Colorado.

Completing a workout at the pool. See, it really is missing.

My son, Forrest. I like to call him "mini-me."

CHAPTER 5

Kim, My Love and Army Wife

I CAME HOME FROM WORK ONE DAY in Fort Hood, Texas, and had an urgent message from my sister. Being a good little brother, I picked up the phone and called her immediately.

"Amy? What's wrong?" I asked, expecting the worst.

Amy responded, "How soon can you get out here?"

"Why?" I asked, with more worry in my voice.

"I met your future wife today!" she pronounced. "When can you come out to meet her? You will love her."

"Amy, I don't have time for this. I don't need a wife. I don't even have time for a girlfriend. I can't even take leave until next year after this deployment is complete."

"Okay, you promised. One year. You better get out here, before she's gone."

■ ■ ■

Amy is my best friend. She and I have been through a lot together. She has always taken care of me. As a child, I still wasn't speaking after the other kids were already forming sentences. My parents took me to speech pathologists and psychologists, but it turned out my problem was simply that I didn't *need* to speak—Amy was doing everything for me. My parents started to figure it out when they saw Amy eating all my food while I sat quietly watching her eat something I didn't like anyway. More important, I *was* talking, but just to Amy. She has always known what I want and what is best for me. She is an incredible sister. Every man needs an angel on his shoulder, and Amy has been that for me.

So, when she told me about Kimberly Batchelor, I knew she was serious. Kim and Amy met working as foresters at the South Carolina Sand Hill State Forest. They spent lots of time together, as they were the only two young single women there. They found over the months that they had tons of things in common. It seemed heaven-sent that two people so much alike would find each other in a place like that.

Six months after Amy's call I called her one night to chat and met Kim over the phone. My sister was out of town, so Kim and I talked with a casual easiness of two old friends. After nearly two hours of conversation, I decided that we did in fact need to meet. But after a few days, I knew how unlikely it would be. Kim remained on my mind even as I left to train in the desert in February 1997.

At the time, I was not very happy. I loved the Army but was missing my freedom on the road. More so, I was lonely. Not the kind of loneliness that makes you sad, but loneliness for friendship. I needed a friend who would challenge me. In my journal, I wrote:

When soldiers talk about home...

Waking up to favorite meals and warm bodies

Puppies rolling on their backs, with tired feet rubbing bellies

Children squeezing thighs with instinctive hugs

Cold beer out of frozen mugs, in rooms lit only by the tellie

I know none of this

I think only of stories I forgot to tell

Waking up to minarets, calling for prayer

Or roosters crowing from orange trees at morning's first light

Swimming the warm currents with the moon lighting the
  ocean floor

Or dancing in the street, during festivals, with numbed smiles;

The light of firecrackers blurred by sangria

These things, I will try to remember next time.

After deploying for two months to the National Training Center in California, I kept my promise to go see my sister for her birthday. Amy conveniently invited Kim to stay with her to celebrate. She announced upon Kim's arrival that I would be arriving the next day. Kim decided to stay.

As I entered, I mistook Kim for my sister and smiled, approaching for a hug. I stopped just short of her, looked into her beautiful eyes, and realized that I had stumbled upon a surprise.

Confused, I took her hand and listened closely to her name. "I'm Kim," she said.

It was then that I heard my sister's laughter from the other room. She announced, "Oh good, you've met Kim. Kim is the girl I've been telling you about."

I had had no idea Kim was going to be there, but I was pleased. Very pleased.

My next journal entry about my visit to Amy was quite different than the one I had written before I left for California:

> I found myself in a driving rain, making my journey home. The rain squelched the summer's early hatchlings of moths and butterflies, which usually litter southern highways and windshields with their confused and misdirected flee from the cocoon. I sped over the ground thinking only of the familiarity of the place my family now considers home. The reunion was the first planned after a year's hard labor.
>
> I entered the door as a traveler who had been lost at sea, bombarded with questions and stories. As I entered, I found a girl who I initially could not recognize from my own sister. Her hair was the spun gold of some treasured spider, while her eyes poured on me the soft rain I had first felt months before.
>
> Her eyes, whose beauty is similar to gems, which the first ocean travelers returned with from voyages, after years of trading treasure, flaunting their most precious cargo. Each was the color of deep, calm seas, and as light as passing clouds. Her shoulders were strong, but with the softest skin.

I stepped away, feeling that I was trapping her with my stare; passing pleasantries I have learned as a cordial man. We sat together and conversations turned to the familiar. I had not sat long before she brought me a bowl of freshly washed grapes.

Once finally alone, I realized how comfortable she had become at the other end of the couch. She had turned her pose, hugging her knee and letting her gold spun hair fall over her left shoulder. She spoke with the easiness of a friend and did not bore me with questions, but spoke a familiar language on subjects we both knew and loved. She sat as a queen would sit watching with pleasure as the jester composed a soliloquy. The couch eventually brought us closer together, as years of use loosened the springs enough for us to fall together in the center. Our eyes, only inches apart. I breathed deep her smell, that of a freshly cut meadow, just before heavy rains. Her breathing was with the easiness of a cat as it sets to bathe and sleep.

Morning crept into daylight, casting long shadows along the floor. Together we will walk hand in hand, helping each other through mountain passes, to find the tallest waterfalls. Together we will watch every day's kaleidoscope sunset. She asked me that night, "What do you think love is?"

I responded, "What else can it be?"

■ ■ ■

I left my sister's home and all of South Carolina with that sick feeling in my stomach. I was in love, and was driving home. Had it been a movie, I would have taken the next exit and appeared at her door with flowers in hand, ready to give up my life to be part of hers. I was headed to Texas to resume my life, and she stayed to continue her own. That may have been it.

A few weeks later, I received the following letter:

Dear David,

I ran through the day as I always do; moving from plot to plot thinking about you. What was strange was that today felt like the first day of fall. It is the beginning of July and I was walking around the woods thinking about romantic fires. The wind was blowing gently; bringing in that peculiar smell, that only fall winds bring. It was ironic to be picking blackberries as I walked to my truck. It made me think of intermediate temperatures, long sleeves and light jackets, mountain colors, and of course, thoughts of the related holidays: Halloween and Thanksgiving, which are holidays of fun and family.

I feel myself being taken back to where I was a kid, and the smell of fall in the air meant that school was coming back. Soon I would find myself standing at the end of my driveway sleepy and feeling awkward at the funny, tingly feeling my legs get because of the sensation brought on by my first long pants I had worn in three months. After school, I would go outside and play. Trying to forget where I had been all day and inevitably had to go back to the next day. I would pretend it was summer and play 'til the sun went down.

I still like to do that. Whenever I get the chance in the fall, I enjoy going on long strolls 'til just before dark. The aura of the time cleanses my soul every time. I hope to be able to walk with you some weekends I spend with you this fall. I say hope only because I hope that we won't be too busy every weekend to take time out to enjoy each other; to talk and hold hands while we walk.

Yours,

Kim

From that point, it was a long-distance, whirlwind courtship. We'd fly back and forth to see each other, even as she moved twice, and filled our weekends with skiing, hiking, camping, generally having lots of fun. Ten months after we met, we went to Mardi Gras in New Orleans for Valentine's Day; I asked Kim to marry me in Jackson Square at the edge of the French Quarter on the waterfront. Down on one knee, lots of tears, the whole show.

We were married within a year. Kim was now an Army wife, but it would be a while before she realized what that meant. We didn't live together for the first two years. One month after we were married, I was off to Kuwait for a six-month rotation. Kim was pursuing her master's of science in forestry, and was happy to have me gone. She already had her undergraduate degree in forest resource management from Clemson University and was now working toward her master's at Stephen F. Austin State University in Nacogdoches, Texas.

With me in Kuwait, Kim could really focus on her studies. But when I returned from Kuwait and had to go to my next level of

training at Fort Knox, Kentucky, it meant another period of separation. Then came my orders for a one-year assignment in Korea. The
day that assignments are posted at the Armor Advanced Course is
referred to as "Day of Woe" because some assignments are not wanted
or expected. They weren't kidding; I had thought I'd get to go to Fort
Carson, Colorado, for the first time. I admit I was angry, especially
after I had just volunteered for a six-month tour in Kuwait, which I
thought would exempt me from another tour overseas. But the Army
needed me to go to Korea to work on war plans, so to Korea I went.

Korea turned out to be a dream assignment for me. The separation was difficult, and we missed each other deeply. But it was helpful—
Kim focused on writing and defending her thesis and I learned how to
plan real-world combat missions while fulfilling my overseas duty
requirement. Kim was able to take a few months off and stay with me
in Korea. Her first true experience in the Army was spending Christmas Day in Seoul in a snowstorm at a hotel with a bunch of Army guys
and a few Army wives. She was able to see for the first time the close-
ness we develop as Army leaders.

We took some interesting trips after Christmas, which we
thought of as a long honeymoon. Our first was to Beijing and the surrounding territories. Kim enjoyed climbing remote sections of the
Great Wall the most. We then spent a few weeks jumping Air Force
cargo flights to get to a rugby tournament in Guam. En route, we had
a "difficult" layover in Okinawa, Japan—not a bad place to be stuck.
There, Kim was able to see me play rugby for the first time. It was
funny, after being married for two years, we were finally getting to
know each other. We flew back and spent a few days in Tokyo. Our

next trip was to Hong Kong and then a few weeks in Thailand, where we enjoyed scuba diving, spelunking, jungle trekking, elephant jungle tours, and beach bumming. Kim really got a good feel for Asia in her few months and an even better feel for me, and then went back to the States to defend her thesis. I stayed in Korea another three months. Her visit really softened our time of separation.

By the time I came back from Korea, the honeymoon was over. The attacks of 11 September had occurred, which put stress as a married couple looking at the prospect of war. But Kim and I also were living together for the first time, and it was a difficult transition. We had been very happy together for short, fun, intimate periods during our long-distance relationship; it didn't require much work. Now we were sharing a small duplex in Fort Carson, Colorado. We were both strong-willed, determined people who, in reality, were just getting to know each other outside of our romance. For two years, we had basically lived a weekend marriage; living together every day makes it tough to overlook bad habits. It was tense.

Once the snow started falling, things got better. We began spending our weekends skiing. We forgot all about what a pain in the ass each had become to the other over the past month. You know, I would leave the toilet seat up and she would overstuff the closet. It also wasn't long before we got new, larger quarters, and we were comfortable again, with both our new space and with each other.

Colorado was a dream come true for us. We spent our summers climbing mountains and camping. We enjoyed winters full of skiing. We lived each day as if it were our last, because we were never sure when my deployment orders would arrive. I had never been so happy.

■ ■ ■

An Army wife has specific duties. In fact, a commander's wife is expected to participate in her husband's career, to the point that a commander and his wife are referred to as a "command team." Being the hardheaded woman that she is, Kim often complained that she wasn't in the Army, and she didn't have to do everything she was told. Her attitude changed as I took command of a cavalry troop and war loomed in the distance. The role of a commander's wife is as the line of communication between the deployed troop and their families.

The relationship of a command team is extremely important, as "deployed" means "war." The Army is a unique organization in the sense that commanders are charged specifically with taking care of their soldiers' families. It is something I take personally. When I deployed to war, I knew every wife and child of my men, and I knew that they were counting on me to bring their husbands and fathers home. In making a stronger bond with my families, I created two different organizations. I was in charge of the Family Readiness Group (FRG), and my wife and Karen Chumbley, the wife of my first sergeant, Phillip, were in charge of the Family Support Group (FSG).

The purpose of the FRG is to maintain compliance with what the Army tells me I have to do to get my soldiers and their families ready for deployment, which includes lots of forms and briefings from civilian agencies. The idea is to prepare families for separation, and then to be able to maintain contact with families once the soldiers are gone. We maintain a chain of concern, a line of communication between families within the troop all the way up to the regimental commander's wife.

The goal of the FSG is precisely that: support. It is a way for interested wives to get together once a month and meet to discuss things they know and help each other. Often the FSG would throw parties for women with birthdays, make hospital visits together, and cook meals for women who might be having a hard time. They loved doing it and were a true blessing when I came back from the hospital after my injury. Kim was nine months pregnant, I was bedridden, but because of these women, we didn't have to lift a finger for two weeks.

Thank you, Karen.

Kim was lucky because I had a first sergeant (the most senior noncommissioned officer in the troop) whose wife was thrilled to run the day-to-day operations. Karen was a lifesaver to Kim, as the soldiers' wives felt more comfortable contacting her. Kim, as an officer's wife, was less approachable. A few of the ladies were intimidated by her position and thought she wouldn't understand them. Karen was able to understand the enlisted wives better than Kim, as she had once been a young enlisted wife herself. During this process, Karen also became a dear friend to both Kim and me. Both Kim and I came to Karen for advice and as a shoulder to cry on every now and then. As far as soldier issues go, it should be no surprise to anyone that our young soldiers marry young. When we got our deployment orders, my married soldier rate went from 20 percent to 70 percent in a matter of weeks. Most soldiers don't want to go off to war without having someone back home. So Kim became a real Army wife because she had to jump in and help these families.

When I found out that I was training with the 10th Mountain Division for Urban Operations, it became clear that we were more and more likely heading to Iraq. Prior to my deployment in October 2002, Kim and I had discussed the impending war. Certainly, our decision to have a child was not decided over one conversation, but there was one night in particular on our back porch that I will never forget. My wife thinks that I remember it with more Southern charm than it may have had, but I remember it clearly.

"David, I am worried about you going to war," Kim said casually, while sipping a glass of merlot.

With a smile, I responded jokingly, toasting my glass, "Yes, Kim, but I am a bad ass, and bad asses don't die!"

"Yes, but what if Saddam decides to use some weapon that may leave you sterile, or affect your nervous system? What if you don't come home?" she said, choking back tears.

More seriously now, I said, "Baby, I am going to make it. Don't worry. I have trained my soldiers. They are lethal. I will come home from this war, victorious."

No longer holding back tears, she said, "I know, but I want to have something left of you if you die. I want to have your baby."

■　■　■

The morning I had to say goodbye was difficult. Due to some political unrest in Turkey (the government wouldn't let U.S. forces invade Iraq from the north), we were now competing for land and air space with the 4th Infantry Division. The 4th ID has a brigade combat team at Fort Carson, which is one-third of the force, with the rest of the division at Fort Hood. We were competing for ports on both ends of the deployment, in the U.S. and in Kuwait. Each time we thought we had a solid date to deploy, we would get bumped. Everyone was out having their last big dinners together for weeks. By the time I had a "no kidding" deploy date, Kim and I were out of money from all our "last dinners." I think on the true "last night" we had leftovers from the previous three "last nights," which were excellent. It was steak, pasta, and vegetables from three different restaurants, but they all went well together over a cold beer.

Through the night, there were no calls to say that the plane had been cancelled or rerouted. The alarm seemed too early at 0300 hours. I took my last shower for the next few months and shaved, savoring the hot water. Kim lay watching me as if I were a reality show on TV. She lay on her side, burdened by a child of six months in her stomach. She was beautiful, like a Roman frieze depicting motherhood. I came and gave her a kiss, because I could.

I dressed with the normal cadence in which I have dressed in the dark a thousand times. This time, though, I dressed ensuring that I had everything: knife, wallet, ID card, dog tags, notecards, pen, glasses, and lighter. As I stood in the kitchen placing the breakfast and lunch sacks Kim had prepared into my backpack, I inhaled the aroma of the brewing coffee. I knew that I would not smell brewing coffee again, maybe for a year. I breathed deeply and thought about all I would miss. Opening my eyes, I saw Kim. It was unusual to have her as part of this common "go to the field" ritual that I had become so accustomed to. But she was there, smiling at me in her pajamas, laughing at my enjoyment and addiction to coffee. She was beautiful.

We had discussed the night before that it would be better if we said goodbye at the house, then had her drop me off with little ceremony just before 0400 hours. So I started the truck and loaded my few last possessions, then returned to the kitchen for my last kiss. As I returned from the car, she was waiting for me with open arms just inside the door. Not a word was spoken, but our lips met in soft kisses, gently salted with tears. As I hugged her one last time, I felt the baby inside her move. I felt the hug of two.

My last kiss in the kitchen was on Kim's belly. We had decided not to find out what the sex of the child was, but I desperately wanted to know. But I thought to myself, "What if I die?"

We didn't speak during the three-mile drive, listening in silence to a CD by Widespread Panic. In my truck in the parking lot, we kissed goodbye as if I were just off to another monthlong field exercise. Inside, I was falling apart. She left to go back home. I went to my office and sat alone, collecting myself for about five minutes. I was ready for war, and Kim was ready to take care of the wives left behind.

I grabbed my holster and walked down to my arms room to draw my pistol and rifle. Yes, I was ready for war.

Saying goodbye is never easy.

CHAPTER 6

An End to Major Combat in Iraq

I T WAS MY SISTER AMY'S BIRTHDAY on 28 April 2003, the day
we crossed into Iraq. It was also the birthday of the country's dic-
tator, Saddam Hussein.

Happy birthday, Saddam. Have we got a present for you, I thought.

It was good to finally march north. The president had given the
order to invade almost a month earlier, in late March. Third Infantry
Division (3rd ID) had led the first attack, along with a Marine expeditionary unit. About 35,000 warriors had been rolling to the capital
for several weeks. We had been left in reserve as reinforcements, to be
brought up to protect the western flank of 3rd ID. Before crossing, we
had spent the two days at the border in horrible sandstorms and even
a few thunderstorms.

Even with orders in hand, it was a race to see which units would get into Iraq first. Third ID was already on the outskirts of Baghdad. Now the goal was to get into the country and fight—before there was no fight left. I was heading in before my men, not on my tank, and into some serious uncertainty. But I was certainly excited about crossing into Iraq. I slept quite well on the roof of my truck, for the three hours I was able to sleep before we started lining up in the dark to roll out.

Just getting the convoy moving was a mess; we had over a hundred pieces of rolling stock. My part of the convoy consisted of about ten recovery vehicles, but would grow to about thirty as we continued to march and came upon broken-down vehicles. We were lined up along the last stretch of highway in Kuwait; which ended in the obstacle complexes that mark Iraq's border. I crossed the border with my driver, Specialist Westman, and my fire support officer, who was also a good friend and bodyguard, First Lieutenant Thomas Whitmore.

We left early in the morning and crossed into Iraq at about 0600 along Highway 8, "The Highway of Death." This is the stretch of highway down which U.S. forces pursued retreating Iraqi forces during the Gulf War. Our tanks gave them a real pounding before stopping to establish a defense across the border. It is 308 miles to Baghdad from the Kuwaiti border, about eighteen hours at tactical speed if driven straight through. It was nearly six hours before we hit our first major town, Al Basrah, and we carefully skirted it. From the time we left the wire at the border patrol station, there were women and children lining the streets waving U.S. flags. It reminded me of the black and white films I had seen as a kid showing the liberation of France from Nazi occupation. It was quite clear that we were now part of history.

Iraq was an immediate change from Kuwait. It truly is the fertile crescent. The landscape drastically changed again once we got within ten miles of the Euphrates. Green grass, palm forests, and sunflowers were a pleasant change for the eye from desert dunes. The weather was also considerably nicer, as it seemed ten degrees cooler as we approached the river. The houses were mainly brick and mud mortar. The villages really did look like scenes you might imagine out of the Bible. The interstate highway system was actually better than ours, with rest stops about every hundred kilometers. Every ten kilometers there were overpasses for camel ranchers and shepherds to allow their livestock to cross. When we would stop for maintenance halts, it seemed that people came out of the sand dunes. We would be two hours from any terrain feature on the map, but as soon as we stopped, locals appeared and were asking for food and water. It was difficult because we wanted to maintain distance between us and any potential enemy, and as they innocently approached, we would have to stop them and search them for weapons. They were confused by our actions, but once searched, they would stand and watch us like we were from outer space.

The road march was a good experience. Along the roads were thousands of people waving and blowing kisses. Samawah was the first town of note past Al Basrah, where we became tense. We tightened up because of all the crowds of people along the roadways and cross streets, and they were not all blowing kisses and waving. We were passing through our first major city at the height of rush hour, and on what must have been market day. Merchants had set up their shops in the streets, and crowds of people often blocked the roadway. You could tell that there were soldiers who had already gone ahead of us, because men walked the streets trying to sell cigarettes and sodas to our boys. It was an embarrassment to me to know that undisciplined soldiers had come ahead of us and bought from the economy. My men were under strict orders to not buy anything. A merchant could roll a grenade into the vehicle or distract the gunner to allow an unobserved attack from the flank. We had reports of those kinds of assaults, and we didn't make any friends in that city. My mission was to pass through with little incident, and that we did.

We spent the night outside Ad Diwaniyah in a hastily established reserve refuel point. We had eight hours to get fixed, fueled, and rested before charging north again. My mechanics worked all night and I eventually had to designate drivers to sleep.

Children who had crawled through the wire were everywhere, watching and trying to sell their now worthless dinar. Soldiers were suckers for the exchange, especially if a child had crisp bills. Currency with Saddam's picture on it was quite a first-day souvenir. I had to repeat my order to the soldiers as we lined up to move out again: no money exchange. I didn't want to take souvenirs away from my soldiers, but the money had no value and our exchange was having a dramatic effect on the community. People were leaving their jobs at the power plant or the marketplace in an attempt to make money from their now worthless notes. It was hard to police, but it had to stop.

The last leg of the march took us along the Euphrates. We settled at an air base next to a giant saltwater lake, Buhayrat Ar Habbaniyah. We camped on the northeast side.

We were now in Iraq. It was monumental. It was a relief to have made it after two days of uncertain travel in new terrain and little intelligence. Although we were relieved to be in a camp, there was no stopping. We had to establish security to defend ourselves until the tanks arrived.

That night we stood on the aircraft bunker and watched the war. To the west, we watched Apaches attack ground troops guarding a weapons depot. We witnessed some dramatic explosions that lit up the western skies. To the north, 82nd Airborne was fighting in Al Habbaniyah. The sky was filled with burning trails of flashing and flying bullets. You could pick out both enemy positions and friendly positions. The insurgents were firing heavy caliber machine guns that used green tracers; we fired red tracers. The big booms were from the helicopters, which were blazing rockets into enemy positions. It was like watching TV back home, but it was real, and it made everyone watching take the war a little more seriously. We were right there. I could smell it.

As we were watching, a runner came with news from our squadron command post that the president had declared an end to major combat in Iraq. It was May 1, just two days after I had gone in.

After this news I reminded my leaders that the next phase of the war was just beginning. Five divisions of Iraqi soldiers had surrendered without a fight as our forces swept into Baghdad. These men were now home, unemployed, defeated, and angry—a bad combination. These men were trained and would be willing to fight for their land, just as we would, with whatever techniques they could employ to have the advantage of surprise. We would go from fighting armies to fighting terrorists. And for us, the rules of war would change—we would have to conduct ourselves with more balanced interaction with locals. From here on out, we might not be able to simply shoot back.

The following day I kicked out with a maintenance team to link up with the other 120 men in my troop. They arrived in nine tanks, thirteen Bradleys, two mortar-tracked vehicles and two support-tracked vehicles filled with parts, tools, and supplies. They arrived at about 2100 local time and we marched back out onto the desert along the highway. It was nice to travel at night because the civilians were obeying the curfew and the highway was clear.

Drivers in the Middle East are crazy. They give themselves the right of way all the time. It is even more dangerous during a war, when there is a complete sense of lawlessness among the people.

We assembled in the desert outside Baghdad for a maintenance break and then finished the road march. The men were tired but worked hard to fix their tanks. They were all so dirty; they had been riding in their hatches atop giant trailers and behind big rigs for three days.

We made it safely to our objective, an abandoned enemy air force base southwest of Baghdad. Besides being hungry for chow, the men were also hungry for information. Although our mission was not yet clear, I was able to brief them on the local threat and potential courses of action. They had been sitting on their vehicles for two days, heading north, and now they wanted to fight. Our first mission was to establish security around the perimeter of the squadron. It took a full day on such a large site.

My commanding officer, Lieutenant Colonel Henry A. "Butch" Kievenaar II arrived. He was commander of 3rd Squadron, codename Thunder 6. He was a battle-hardened veteran of the first Gulf War, tough and decisive. We were glad to have him there to lead us.

After a week in camp, our vehicles and men were ready. We begged for missions and found ourselves guarding a mass gravesite. Fortunately, we were relieved from the gravesite rather quickly, frustration began to set in. Although it was important evidence for possible war crime trials, we all thought we would be doing more in Iraq than guarding gravesites. Third ID had been so successful in reaching Baghdad with no counterattack that we were several weeks ahead of the invasion plan. Not even the war planners back at Central Command (CENTCOM) had anticipated this; they were working furiously at all levels to catch up to the situation on the ground.

We finally got orders to move north and establish a new camp three kilometers north of Hit, along the Euphrates. The first step was getting there. This time I would be on my tank and commanding my troops in battle. We conducted the 120-kilometer tactical road march across the desert with little effort. Besides some minor maintenance trouble, it was your usual road march.

The Republican Guard tank-training base we occupied was full of rubble, but a day's work had things spic-and-span. We didn't have power or water, but we did have some overhead cover. Judging by the graffiti and images on the wall, it appeared we were residing in barracks intended for soldiers. Propaganda was all over the camp: painted images of U.S. flags burning, U.S. flags with the star of David, and graffiti like "Down with U.S.A." It was a large camp with everything an

Arab might need: mosque, school, PT grounds, parade field, and rifle range. We even were able to learn a little about their training by studying the facilities around the camp. It was interesting to see that they trained a lot like us. The camp was much more modern than I had expected. We were right on the banks of the Euphrates and far enough out of town to maintain a safe distance from the local people. I was pleased with my decision, considering that I had picked the site off a map, which is often a risk. The camp still had most of its original wire around the perimeter, so all we had to do was occupy it and establish security.

Best of all, we had a combat mission. We were assigned an area of operation that included three relatively large cities. Hit was the biggest, the tribal and religious epicenter for several towns and surrounding communities. It was also the regional Ba'ath party headquarters. Our mission was to establish safety and security for the Iraqi people. There were obstacles: no maps, no intelligence, and no translators. Also, we were the first American forces in the town. So we were starting from scratch; we had no previous informants or even the names of those in power. The scouts reported no waving flags or happy children in the streets. Rather, the town was shut down. These people had wealth, but nobody was working. The only people seen were those peeking through windows.

I was now in charge of a part of Iraq, and was ready to start making a difference.

CHAPTER 7

First Contact

O N 7 MAY 2003, WHILE ON MY FIRST PATROL in Hit, I had my first direct contact with the enemy. My first inter- action with the people of Hit was much more entertaining than I like to admit.

I was riding in my Humvee escorted by two other gun trucks. We were conducting a patrol of the city for reconnaissance and to create a working map of the area. We entered the town through a roundabout and headed east towards the town center. As we drove down the main street, the street filled with spectators and people on motorcycles and cars began to crowd our convoy. We crawled along, trying to record the main streets in a good sketch. I also needed to determine which roads were navigable by our different classes of vehicles. Some streets were impassable by our tanks, as they were much too narrow. The tanks might also collapse existing bridges and culverts in some streets. I eventually saw a road that would need to be driven and surveyed. I called for my driver to go left. As he had already missed the turn, he slammed on the brakes. I heard the sound of an impact behind me and turned to find a confused Iraqi man sprawled in the back of my truck. He had been following too close on his motorcycle and was launched into the back of my truck when he collided with us. I jumped out, pulled him free, and set him on the ground. And that is how I met my first Iraqi. No shots fired.

The mission improved from there. I was going to be able to go back and draw a fairly good map to plan future operations in and around the city. We were completing our last few planned routes when we passed an intersection on the edge of town where I noticed a group of men passing around weapons, mainly rifles. Then I thought I heard small arms fire. My standing orders were to disarm anyone with a weapon. I radioed in a report to my higher headquarters back at the base.

"Thunder, this is Killer 6. I have identified a group of men passing around weapons."

"Roger, Killer, disarm and report."

"Killer, this is Killer 6. I want Blue platoon to the east in a blocking position, and Roach to the west in a blocking position. As soon as the blocking positions are set, I want a section of dismounts to establish security, and another to move in to disarm and search vehicles."

"Blue, Roger."

"Roach, Roger." (This was Brown platoon, nicknamed "Roach" since roaches are brown.)

I took a deep breath and thought, "This is it."

I responded, "Okay, Killer, here we go."

We pulled in and blocked both intersections with my two gun trucks. I guided my vehicle in between the two intersections and stood outside my Humvee with two hand mikes, a hand-held radio, binoculars, and a rifle on my hood in the middle of what turned out to be a gun market. Men were selling weapons from the trunks of half a dozen cars; there was even a table full of guns set up next to an animal pen. I assessed the situation and quickly developed a plan of action.

Bullets suddenly whizzed over my head. One of my lieutenants called in, "Shots fired!"

I tried to move my dismounts into better positions, but the gunmen were firing as they fled through the crowded streets.

Over the handheld radio, I ordered, "Roach, we are establishing a supporting position here, try to move down the next street and regain direct contact."

In anger and haste, I found myself moving away from the vehicle to better see the array of forces. I was walking and not using cover as I moved down the street. The gunmen continued to fire in my direction. Sergeant First Class McNichols grabbed me by the shoulder and pulled me to the ground.

"Sir, what the fuck are you doing?" he yelled.

"That fucker is trying to kill me and he's getting away!" I responded.

"Goddamn it, sir, you can't give me orders if you are dead," he said, looking into my eyes.

I was screwing up. I was trying to do it myself and was walking into a firefight. I moved back to my vehicle and asked for a situation update from my leaders.

"Killer, SITREP!" (Situation report.)

"This is Blue. I have established an over watch and am clearing this street north. Negative contact. These guys just disappeared."

"Roger."

"This is Roach. I have a team moving down the street, and cannot regain contact. I am leaving two men to guard you and control the crowd."

I stopped to check my forces and saw hundreds of townsfolk at each of my blocking positions. We had too few men to conduct this raid, but I wanted to try to regain contact with the insurgents.

"Roger, Roach and Blue, continue to march and report."

As the men reacted to my orders, I observed one man dressed in black with a black head wrap covering all but his eyes. He continued to walk down the street calmly firing an AK-47 at me. My driver was busy firing flares with his M203 to signal the Kiowa helicopters for support, so I took aim with my rifle. But the man in black was surrounding himself with women and children. As he walked, he would order them to surround him.

The future relationship with the city we would be working in for the next year hung in the balance. It was a mere fingertip's pull away. In an instant, I decided it was more important to establish myself as the American leader in the city rather than risk shooting a woman or child in harm's way and alienating the whole community on my first day in town, perhaps even triggering an uprising.

I let him walk away, knowing I probably let a terrorist escape.

■ ■ ■

Within minutes, we established security in the market. The situation returned to normal. People went back to going about their business. After fifteen minutes, we returned to camp.

When we got back, I huddled with my leaders. We talked about how to do things better. Most important, how were we going to shut the gun market down? I had to get these weapons off the street, out of the hands of terrorists. There were so many cached weapons and munitions from abandoned army facilities that it seemed impossible. But we came up with a plan of action and I briefed the boss.

We immediately began to conduct traffic control points (TCP) to search cars coming into the city to ensure that they were not transporting weapons. It was a unique experience because we had to work with the Iraqi police from Hit. Coordinating this was no small feat. By now, we had hired some local translators, but just explaining an operation to them was difficult. The first time I went in to discuss a TCP, I had an interesting conversation.

"Captain, we are not really a police force, like you see on American television. We are more like your constables. We merely oversee the markets and domestic disputes," the fat police chief told me.

The chief was too well manicured to have been suffering under Saddam, so I immediately distrusted him. He wore the uniform of a police officer, but would often come into work in his robes. He was six feet tall, mustached, with dark skin and dark hair, about 220 pounds, and had a large belly. He wore glasses to read, and squinted when he did not have them on. He always looked down when he spoke, but looked at you when you spoke.

I laughed at him and said, "Colonel, I cannot establish law and order in this town with constables. I am also not going to pay your soldiers if all they do all day is smoke cigarettes and eat ice cream on the steps of the station."

He cut his eyes at me and said, "I am the police chief, and have control of this town."

I returned his look and said, "No, this is my town, and I am allowing you to be police chief. This may be your last day of work. The choice is yours."

The chief decided to comply and sent out a patrol with us that afternoon. We established two checkpoints, one north and one south of town. The first vehicle we stopped at the southern checkpoint was the motherload; we seized two AK-47s, three RPGs with eight rockets and penetrators, a complete 60 mm mortar, and about a thousand rounds of AK ammunition. A few more vehicles there had ammo. At the northern checkpoint, we found only one vehicle carrying AK-47s.

We were disappointed because we knew there were more weapons out there—a lot more. Even though these people had no way of communicating, no phones or radios, we concluded that word had gotten out. We assumed an informant network had started because of the significant decrease in traffic on the highway that day. But we were too late anyway. As I drove to the first checkpoint, I looked to town. I could see the cars lined up, open for business. The dealers saw me, slammed their trunks closed, and scattered before we could get to them. They ran deep into the heart of the city. I realized that trying to plan missions was going to be difficult because the dealers were fast and unpredictable, setting up at different times. We would never be able to establish a pattern our intelligence people could count on.

It turned into a game. As I would leave one checkpoint for the other, the dealers would break down and speed away, and then return and set up again after I left. Unfortunately, we couldn't call in air support—scout helicopters with machine guns—because by the time they got there, the dealers would be gone. Finally, my first sergeant and I decided to drive into the market and conduct a raid on our own. The hasty raid was heart-pounding as we both took the wheels and let our drivers dismount to conduct the search and seizure. We each drove with one hand and had our pistols, M-9 Berettas, hanging out the windows in the other. The dealers were gone by the time we pulled up, but had left ten boxes of ammo. The children and crowd stayed to watch us work. My mini-raid was a little cowboy-like, but I got my message across. I was not afraid. From this raid and others, I got my first nickname from the troop, "Kowboy 6." After many raids, the police recognized my determination and finally started to show up to help disperse the crowds.

It is difficult to disarm people, especially civilians who might need weapons to protect themselves and their families. Highway bandits were becoming more prevalent every day. But it was even more difficult to catch those who intended to do harm.

At this point, about a week into my command and after a week of raids, I was not a popular fellow in town. Sometimes when I passed by, people would run out of storefronts and flash the soles of their feet at me. It is an Arab sign of disrespect, and an insult. My men began to assign me extra guards to both protect me from harm and keep me from running right into it.

■　■　■

We finally took down the weapons market. Or at least, what was left of it after the local police tipped off the dealers. Using almost the entire troop, we conducted a synchronized raid from four separate corners and isolated the market. We sent a team out early, as if it were setting up a traffic control point, then had them double back to establish road-blocks to the east. Simultaneously, we closed down the west with the two other teams. Just outside town I established a quick reaction force of tanks with medics as a reinforcing element. We closed the place down. It was beautiful. As we rode in, I crossed a field behind a Bradley and sunk my Humvee to the chassis in sewage mud. The situation was ironic, because it was a perfect place for me as far as my men were con-cerned. To them, I was safe and sound, one less thing to worry about.

After the seizure, we found no weapons but did find cached rifle ammunition and another large stash of propellant, along with eight sticks of dynamite and crates of DETT cord with blasting caps. These were all intended to make roadside bombs.

Zero shots fired. Zero injuries. Bottom line: mission accom-plished.

Despite some butterflies in a few of the men, everyone was pumped up. That day I was named sheriff of Hit, and the sheriff never sleeps.

My first mission as sheriff was to fire the police chief. I had pur-
posely not told the chief about the raid ahead of time. Before I arrived
at the police station, I had my men move to concealed positions short
of the market. Once I knew they were in place, I stopped by to give the
chief a heads-up on the ongoing mission. As soon as I was inside the
station and told the chief my plan, I noticed him quietly dispatching a
man in plainclothes, who was always hanging around, but who was
never introduced to me. My driver watched him leave the building and
jump into a white Toyota SUV. My scouts picked him up and saw him
drive into the gun market and start dispersing the vendors. Upon that
report, I called for the attack to begin. As soon as the raid was complete,
I was back in the police station to send our crooked constable home.

I barged into his office and said, "The vendors were tipped off!
You are through."

He seemed unconcerned and said, "These are people just trying
to make a living."

Looking into his squinted eyes, I said angrily, "I hope it's lucra-
tive, because you're done here."

After briefing my boss, he called together the senior chiefs of the
region and had him removed.

He and his secret police were last seen packing up and heading to
Baghdad. I was happy to see him go. Good riddance.

■ ■ ■

Starting a new police force was my next big challenge. Unfortunately,
their hours of operation (0800–1400 and 1800–2200) did not correspond

with the hours of operation of the criminals. The force was also full of dirty cops.

We started to have a real effect on the people without firing shots at them, even though they were firing at us daily. We started arresting the bad guys. The gangsters appeared to be off the streets and markets were open again. People were getting back to living and were now living free. It was too early for many of them to know what that meant. I felt like we were doing a job that would help the people of Hit and its surrounding municipalities.

We continued working with the local police, despite the corruption. Although they were making some progress in our traffic control points, they were still more interested in not upsetting the locals—and in getting time off.

By the end of May, I felt that our presence was making a difference to the people of Hit. If anything, they were learning that we were not warmongers, but rather that we had good intentions. We started conducting patrols on foot to increase our visibility in the towns. People began to be receptive and happy to see us in markets throughout the area.

■ ■ ■

After maintaining a new training matrix, I took the men out for some tank training. After all our dangerous missions, it was meant to be a sort of break and a little fun. Instead, we experienced our first rocket artillery attack.

In the desert, one of White platoon's scouts reported, "Sir, there are six Bradleys hauling ass right towards us. Are they attacking something?"

No, they were running for their lives. As the Bradleys came toward our position, we could hear and see enemy mortars landing and exploding around them. After a few rounds came close to one of our Bradleys, the driver moved out. Just as he left, a rocket landed and exploded on his old position.

They were bracketing, adjusting their fire to find the targets. That's not something an untrained insurgent would do—these were professional enemy artillerymen. As the Blue platoon moved north, so did the fire. We were watching the attack in awe from a hilltop, not quite believing what we were seeing. We had been told the enemy didn't have the capability to fire rockets anymore. But the mood changed quickly as rockets started landing around us. My last command to rally at my location changed as one rocket exploded closer than fifty meters to our east.

A sandstorm blew up just at that moment. I sent my tanks south to establish a checkpoint on the highway, in case the enemy fled with their equipment. With sand now blowing violently, our visibility was between ten meters and hand-in-front-of-face range. It was the most dangerous move of my career—we could have been run over by one of our own vehicles blinded by the storm, or they could have run into each other. Once south, we stopped to search two men on the side of the road with a motorcycle hidden behind a concrete platform. After finding a shotgun and AK-47, they admitted that two other men with rifles had taken off, running west.

We continued west and established our checkpoint. After arresting a man with a grenade and seizing lots of ammo and a few more rifles, we took fire from the south. It was just harassing fire, but it got our nerves up. A platoon sergeant also had to fire a warning shot to stop one truck. I saw the frustration in the eyes of my men. All that work and only a few unrelated arrests. We had missed our suspects and my guys needed to decompress. It was a long day, and we moved back to establish an assembly area out in the desert for a night of security and some rest. The storm blew all night, so we didn't get much rest. Then we headed back to the base to repair and tune up our vehicles.

We spent the day hiding out from the sandstorm. As we watched *Saving Private Ryan* on a television in the barracks, I thought about the events of the past month. After such a hectic day, reality set in. The most unsettling realization was that there were a lot of people trying to kill me every time I left camp. I had been shot at directly with small arms three times and by rockets and mortars once. Even small attacks could kill or injure me and my men. We had expected to die nobly in battle, in our tanks—not from a stray bullet. The reality also sunk in that I had, on several occasions, had to point loaded weapons at people and had to make decisions about their lives in a matter of seconds. The feeling of pointing a weapon at another man to possibly take his life is a powerful and disturbing feeling.

I continued to try to answer one of my inquisitive lieutenants, who always asked, "What are we doing here?" We had freed the Iraqi people and were now keeping the peace. It was violent work. I trained the men every day, and they were ready. But this place was so fragile, a real powder keg. My only hope each day was that my men would continue to perform their jobs with professionalism and self-control. I was so proud of my troop.

With these thoughts in mind, I scribbled a translation of my feelings into my journal:

Like many men before me, I have come to the desert to pray and understand myself.

I come knowing little in life . . . I come with cleansed hands and an open heart.

I know that meditation in a place without distraction creates single-mindedness; pure thinking.

I think myself not unlike the man who sat in the pew in front of me, years ago; shaking and cursing, unable to relax in a place of worship and solitude.

I can recognize and relax in this place of solitude, where other men cry out in absence, seemingly, of anything real.

I can scream only to hear myself echo; low and deep from canyon walls . . .

Although my voice is not the manifestation of angels, my sound is boisterous; shouting for freedom and praise.

My last lesson before entering the desert was the meaning of Hallelujah; amazing grace, the hour I first believed.

■　■　■

Then everything went to shit.

I had been on the ground surveying a future weapons turn-in site when my radioman called me back to the vehicle.

"Sir, there is some confusing traffic," he said casually.

Expecting some change in location for my weapons turn-in site, I said, "Well, crank it up. Let's head back to base."

Reaching for the radio, I made sure I was loaded with all my men. As we moved out, I radioed, "Last calling station, this is Killer 6."

"Killer 6, this is Thunder 6D [the commander's driver], we are at the police station, and there is a riot outside. Thunder 6 [Lieutenant Commander Kievenaar] wants you to come secure the location and extract some key personnel."

"This is Killer 6, roger."

"Killer 6, this is Killer 5." It was Jon Kluck, my executive officer. I knew something was wrong when he came on.

"Killer 6 . . . Send it."

"Sir, the colonel is in the building with the sheik and there is a serious riot outside. Small arms have been fired at the building, and several police vehicles have been turned over and set on fire."

My commander, Colonel Kievenaar, was at the police station to discuss the fate of a suspect in an RPG attack with the newly appointed mayor of Hit.

"Roger, I am en route with my reconnaissance force to establish security."

As we turned the roundabout and headed to the police station, I could already see the smoke from the burning vehicles and the masses of people all along the street. A few men were dragging improvised obstacles out into the asphalt in an attempt to keep us out. An armed man pushed an obstacle into the street that was intended to flip or severely damage a vehicle and its occupants. Clearly, this had been planned.

I sent a message about my willingness to use force in a seriously dangerous situation by shooting the man dragging out the obstacles. It was the first time I had killed a man. But I didn't have time to think about it. As we turned the last bend, there were over a thousand rioters shooting into our convoy and pelting us with rocks, bricks, and pipes.

I looked over my shoulder at a platoon sergeant in the seat behind me. He looked into my eyes and said, "Sir, what the fuck. . . ."

My driver looked at me and said, "Where the fuck do I go?"

I looked into the crowd and said, "Right through them . . . to the front doors!" I started shooting at a man with a weapon.

My pistol jammed and I looked into the back seat, at one of my platoon leaders, and yelled at him and my driver, "Shoot, goddamn it, shoot!"

But the platoon leader's hand and arm were covered with blood. He was taking direct hits from rocks and metal objects. His trigger finger was ripped open; he couldn't hold his gun. Between his injury and the driver stuck driving, the whole left side of the vehicle was vulnerable. I continued to fire.

I turned toward my driver and yelled, "Turn this motherfucker around and face the crowd. Then get your rifle out and secure this vehicle!"

As I turned back to look out the window, a man was running up to smash me in the face with a cinder block. As he was heaving it toward me through my window, I shot him clean in the chest. He fell away from the truck.

As soon as the vehicle stopped, I yelled, "Establish security, push them back!"

Roach knew exactly where to go and started to lay some suppressing fire with one team while he placed another. I didn't have to give him any orders.

But there was one insurgent behind the platoon sergeant, shooting at them from behind. I could see him, but they could not; he was hiding behind a wall. "What a shitty day to not bring my rifle," I thought to myself in a moment of sick humor.

Though he was fifty meters away, I took aim and shot six rounds at him. All six made white craters in the blue wall behind him, like something out of the comics. I took a deep breath and dropped him with my seventh shot.

Once we pushed back the crowd, there was a moment of silence. I grabbed the platoon sergeant who had ridden with me and went into the building to extract our commander. As I ran in the door, hot AK-47 shells rained down on me. One of the Iraqi cops grew some balls and was firing at the opposing gunmen from the roof. It was an apprehensive feeling to have a former enemy firing above me, but he was now one of my men. I was uneasy, yet relieved.

I ran upstairs, pouring with sweat. Taking a knee, I looked the colonel in the eye and said, "Sir, we have pushed back the crowd, QRF is en route, and I am ready to take you back to camp."

He calmly responded, "How secure is the building?"

"Once the QRF is on site, I can hold it as long as you need. But it may get messy if the mob forms again."

"Roger. Hold your ground and keep me informed."

Those eleven men fought like hell. They held their positions for over a half hour before Bradley reinforcements arrived in support. All of the soldiers fought with great restraint, pushing back over a thousand rioters without civilian deaths or unnecessary injury. Their bravery was pure and as real as it gets in war. I was so proud. For their valorous actions, they all received Bronze Star medals.

But the fight had just begun. As the reinforcements arrived and a platoon leader hit the ground out of the back of the Bradley, a well-thrown grenade went off and sent him down. Another soldier, Private First Class Moyle, who was emplacing a machine gun, ran to him and carried him to my position for medical treatment. I was trying to create a 360-degree perimeter around the police station, so I had to treat the lieutenant myself. As I was treating the shrapnel in his eye and neck, I told Moyle to secure my rear and make sure no other grenades came over the wall.

After I called in a medical evacuation request on the radio, I brought Moyle back to my position to guide in the ambulance. As Moyle approached, I noticed blood soaking through his body armor. I inspected him and saw that he had also taken shrapnel in the neck during the grenade attack. Although only a young private, he had the courage and selfless service to carry another man to safety, without considering his own safety or injury. For his actions, he was awarded the Bronze Star Medal with Valor. My only regret is that I was injured before I was able to award it to him myself.

There were many acts of courage and valor at the police station that day, but the actions of the initial eleven soldiers, and especially the actions of Private First Class Moyle, represent all soldiers and their undying bravery.

During the first steady break we got that day from the unruly crowd, I ordered water to all my dismounted men from the five-gallon cans on each of the reinforcing vehicles. I took a break as well and shared a cigarette with one of my platoon sergeants. As I took my first drag, I noticed my soldiers' blood on my arms and hands. It was also all over the hand-grips of my pistol. A cold chill covered my body; my break was over.

We defended that police station for over six hours before my squadron commander called for our withdrawal. He agreed to turn the city back to the sheiks. Although we withdrew without incident, the helicopters that were providing overhead support reported that over twenty-one grenades and numerous small arms were fired as the enemy again stormed the Hit police station and federal buildings.

That night, I returned to camp just in time to attend a meeting. Near the end, my commander asked me to brief everyone on lessons learned from the day's battle. It was the first moment I had to reflect on what had happened: I was the first officer in the squadron to engage in close combat. I had killed. I gave a standard brief about the mission, but in the back of my mind, I was thinking about what had really happened. I was upset. As a Christian, I had thought before the war about the possibility that I might have to kill. It went against everything I had been taught.

After the meeting, I returned to my quarters. For the first time since coming to Iraq, I prayed for myself, rather than just for my family. I didn't sleep well for the next four nights.

Yes, I had to kill. This was war. It was their lives or mine. It was the craziest experience I'd ever had—like a living nightmare. But all of my men, the commander, and I were alive to fight another day.

After a few days of reflection, 4 June 2003, I wrote Kim and Boo (still a surprise and not yet Forrest) a letter:

Dearest Kim,

As our anniversary approaches, I wanted to give you a special gift. I think my greatest gifts have been those of my words. As I began to write, I could only think of the child you carry for us. What a burden to bear. My sadness is complicated by my desire to be home for the birth, and knowing I will not be there for you.....It pains me to know that I am not going to be home to do my part. For that I am sorry.

As a gift though, I thought of a poem that I would whisper softly to the baby in hopes of sleep. It is written with all my love. I wanted to write something that I would say to Boo all his life; something that I would read at Boo's wedding to remind Boo of our love and commitment. I am not sure if it is going to do any good for helping Boo rest, but it is the least I can do from here. I can hardly wait to be home to read it myself.....I hope though that you read it with me in mind, and the tone and tempo become clear in your voice. I also hope you enjoy it and know how much I care.

I am crazy missing you. I wish I could see you with the baby. I am sure by now you have given up trying to hide it. I can just see you now in your cute little maternity clothes trying to do your chores. I wish I was home to help pick things up, lift, and reach those top shelves for you.

I miss and love you. Enjoy the poem.

Love,

David

<u>TO BOO</u>

Oh come now, my sweet nightingale

Take thy throne on the windowsill

The day has been long; nightfall has come

Day's work is finished, and we're all home

The baby lays awake, but is tired

Growing more each day, its soul still fired

Oh, sing us a sweet lullaby

A melody that will heavy the eye

Sing about heaven, and dancing angels

Soft like snowfall, but warm as summer breezes

Hum softly, like a delicate hand across a harp

Yes, it's working, keep singing, slowing that little heart

Now rest easy my child, we will watch over you

For the rest of your life, our love will protect you

Love,

Dad

CHAPTER 8

Success of the Model City and Its Fall

FTER THE LAST FEW GRUELING WEEKS of fighting, my squadron commander gave the sheiks an ultimatum: Get the city under control or we will declare martial law. They agreed, so we gave them a few days to restore order. That gave us a break.

I rested my men, took a week to focus on maintenance of our vehicles and weapons, caught up on sleep, and got some uniforms washed and changed. Then we were out in force again, searching the terrain along the opposite bank of the Euphrates for possible mortar firing positions. We had received numerous mortar attacks, and they always happened just before a sandstorm. Insurgents fired when they knew our helicopters weren't flying, which meant we were less likely to counterattack. Just before a sandstorm was their best bet. As we were positioned on the banks of a river, they could fire over the river, making themselves difficult to catch. But besides disarming a few men, we were not making the progress we needed.

Since it was becoming obvious that we were not going to catch them in the act, we were ordered to establish weapons turn-in sites throughout the region, with complete amnesty. Getting the message out was hard. We had the message announced from the minarets and had piles of leaflets and information bulletins printed. As we hung them up, my soldiers reported back that a group of civilians were tearing them down. The psychological operations (PSYOP) mission was failing from the start. To combat this, we hung them from midnight to four in the morning. In Iraq, at the end of May, 0001–0400 is the most crowded time of day, as it was the coolest. My men got to the first turn on their route by midnight and received direct fire ten minutes after.

It became obvious that our daily missions were becoming more and more dangerous. Rather than just defending their gun markets, the insurgents were now fighting from rooftops in coordinated attacks. On each mission, we had to be more and more creative in how we provided force protection. It became almost unreasonable to go into the city, day or night, without aircraft for support.

We did establish a weapons turn-in site, much to the chagrin of my noncommissioned officers. My senior NCOs had run programs like this in Bosnia and Kosovo; they believed that the only way it would work would be if we offered locals something in trade like money or food. They were right, but I had my orders. My unit did not yet have the money or the authority to establish a weapons-for-cash program.

The idea was to establish a military amnesty point outside a city where citizens could turn in any illegal weapons they were storing in their homes. It was quite common for the average citizen to have RPGs and assault rifles. Even more common were the piles of unexploded ordnance people would store in their homes, processing the copper and metal from the rounds for money. This left hundreds of pounds of highly explosive propellant in people's kitchens—or worse, in their backyards in the sun. The propellant is so unstable that there were many incidents of people blowing themselves up.

For a week, Blue platoon ran the weapons turn-in point south of Hit. Covered by two Bradleys, it had two pits for weapons and ammo. It was a "total amnesty" point; we didn't detain anyone or even check identification. But by the end of it, we had only a handful of blank ammunition to show for our work. It seemed a waste of time, but it did allow us to be stationary inside the city and observe more of the traffic throughout the day. I treated it as a scout mission; we learned a lot about traffic patterns and the schedule of the city.

During the first week of the turn-in, a local man stopped by and yelled out in nearly perfect English, "If you were to give money in return for weapons, I know you would get most of them off the streets."

He, like my NCOs, was correct. But money was not yet available. And we also knew that bandits and highway robbers would be the only ones making money, as they had plenty of spare weapons to turn in, and we would be supporting them. Most Iraqis don't give something for nothing. We also confused things by allowing each man in the home to retain one rifle to protect his family. (That law became problematic for us, especially considering that people were shooting at us from their own homes.) Our best source of leads on weapons stashes was children. They'd often bring boxes of grenades, belted ammunition, or blasting caps to trade for MREs (our "meal ready to eat" rations in plastic pouches). It was not our preferred method for weapons turn-in, but my soldiers were suckers for the kids.

A few days after the turn-in operation ended, one of our interpreters came to camp to visit us. We made sure to pay him well, as his information was often good. When we had first set up camp, Mr. Ali had been brave enough to come to our front gates and beg to help us. He had spent three years in medical school; we called him "Doc." (He was the informant who eventually alerted me to the price on my head.) After checking him out with intelligence services, and acting on a few reliable tips, we found him to be trustworthy and made him part of the team. And we paid him well—$10 a day. After a few visits to camp, he revealed that he was building an information network in town. As his information continued to pan out, we increased his payoffs to $20 a day. That's the gross monthly income for a typical Iraqi. Within a few days, he was bringing eyewitnesses to camp to describe certain targets for us and answer specific questions about them. We sometimes even sent our own scouts with them, hidden in Iraqi vehicles to better photograph target houses and areas. Our arrests became higher and higher in value.

Doc was a well-dressed and well-educated man who dressed in western style, always in a plaid shirt, and wore expensive shoes. He looked no different from a typical Iraqi, but he smiled and carried himself much more upright, and also had less of a gut. He looked like a soccer player and walked around with the swagger of one. Doc spoke English with a perfect British accent, as he had been educated in a British university. He was incredibly important to us.

One day, Doc said, "We know there are a group of men who have adopted all black garments who intend to take a stand in the city. They call themselves 'The Sons of Saddam.' They are planning in the mosques at evening prayer and are deployed throughout the city the rest of the night. The cleric has told them they will be paid $1,000 for the life of any American."

We started pounding him with questions. We'd seen these guys before—one of them, I believe, was the man at our first raid who had surrounded himself with women and children to escape. But he responded, "This is all I know, I am very sorry."

With this new intelligence, my commander decided that we needed to increase mounted and dismounted patrols in the city and resume observation twenty-four hours a day. We had been running traffic control points north and south of camp from 2100–2400 in expectation of an attack. But we found few weapons and experienced no attacks. We didn't want an attack, of course, but these TCPs tied up a lot of manpower and yielded little. Same thing for our patrols of known smuggling routes and our searches of passing cars. The bad guys knew we were looking for them, so they just stayed put. Instead we ended up searching mostly innocent farmers.

It was only a few weeks before the sheiks assured us that they were back in power, and were prepared to elect a police chief and a mayor. Even with this news, we weren't going back into the city until it was a bit safer. It felt like a trap. Once the local police were reestablished we would go in and force a curfew. Then things would really get interesting.

As the sheiks met in private to establish a new mayor and police chief, I again dedicated some time to my men. The men were doing fine and continued to adjust to their new life in Iraq. You must keep a soldier busy or he will get bored, and boredom results in trouble. Missions make them happy, especially when they're dangerous. Everyone wants some action.

With the approaching summer, we tried to adjust to the Arab summer day. The locals slept all day and worked all night. For us it seemed impossible. It was so, so hot. Basically, we would just lie on our cots and sweat all day, then work at night. We were each averaging about thirty minutes of sleep a day, then trying to squeeze in another nap sometime during the cool evening. But it seemed like every time I would try to lie back and sleep, we would get attacked by mortar fire. I became tired and frustrated, which is not a good mix. It took a couple of weeks to transition to a complete reverse cycle.

But the monotony of things changed on 10 June, when we went back into the city to enforce the curfew. The curfew in place was scheduled throughout the remainder of June from 2400 to 0300, the time identified as the most common period for terrorist attacks. We conducted a three-day PSYOP campaign to get the word out. On the night of 8 June, the mortars and fire support team went into town to hang flyers, but quickly returned after getting shot at in another coordinated attack from both ground and rooftop. Rather than just hanging flyers, we depended on the PSYOP team to send the message out by driving through town blasting the message through loudspeakers mounted on their Humvees. We continued to drive the streets, even under an occasional hail of fire and bullets.

Our message (recorded in Arabic), was simple: "We cannot tolerate the terrorist attacks against our soldiers as we try to protect your city. Due to recent events, Hit is under curfew. Violators will be arrested, and anyone carrying a weapon will come under attack. Please remain in your homes between midnight and three o'clock in the morning. Curfew will continue until further notice"

After three days and nights of message playing, we were ready again to enforce the curfew. It had taken only a week for the sheiks to elect a new mayor. He was the young son of the most powerful sheik in the region. The new police chief was his brother. As their family had one-third of the vote, it was a fairly easy election.

Well, the word about the new, strong leadership from the most powerful tribe in the region got out, but was not quite understood by the insurgents. The good news was that the new mayor and chief of police wanted things to work. The new chief quickly began to recruit a police force, made up mainly of former Iraqi soldiers and local young men who were out of work and looking for jobs. As an act of goodwill between the new mayor and my commander, they both went on patrol with me through Hit. We made sure we stopped at certain places along the way, so that the people of his town saw his cooperation. He was not scared, but had a fairly large entourage of bodyguards.

On our first curfew enforcement, all hell seemed to break loose. As we arrived, crowds formed immediately. I called for the PSYOP guys to come and broadcast the curfew message. Of course, it took some force to keep the crowd at bay. With a new police force, now at

120 men, we thought we'd have no problem manning the sites and patrols. Unfortunately, they work day on–day off cycles, so we only had sixty men on hand to choose from. None were in uniform, and at times, it was difficult to distinguish between the police and the bad guys.

It was a little tense, especially considering the mayor and the commander were there under my security and watch. We finally separated out the police and started issuing weapons. It felt odd, considering that some of them were former Iraqi soldiers. We were doing something quite historic. We were issuing weapons to Iraqi soldiers just one month after the war. Fortunately, my worries were in vain, as the men were excited to have a job and to enforce the curfew. Still, it was a unique feeling to walk down the streets with armed Iraqi soldiers.

The first night went quite well. Not too many problems, and only a few people out as we returned to the market before turning back to the police station. At the beginning of the march, a man had thrown a grenade toward us, but it went off without injury to anyone. Toward the end of our march, there was some small arms fire from a rooftop, but we could not give up our security posture and pursue. We lost two weapons—or rather, there were two weapons not returned. It seemed that the sheik's bodyguards were building their armory.

The second night was a little more interesting. As we prepared for the mission and issued weapons, we again realized that we had a new crew of police and leaders. We worked through the pain of training a ragtag police force a second night in a row. But then a potential problem showed up. The number-one wanted man from our local blacklist, a high-ranking Sunni cleric, walked into the police station and offered to help us.

I knew something was up when my interpreter, one of my first sergeants, started eavesdropping on the loud conversation in the station. He whispered to me, "Captain, I think there is something wrong."

I could tell by the look on his face that there was indeed something wrong, and said, "Well?" He strained to listen without being obvious.

"The men (police) are talking about a criminal who wants to walk with you through town tonight," he said calmly, but with sweat running down his face.

"Get his name," I said and paused to call on my radio for a runner. "Roach, this is Killer 6. Send a runner to my location."

The young private appeared at the door as if I had said a magic spell. "Stand by," I barked, not trying to cause any suspicion.

Looking at my interpreter, I asked again, "Well?"

As soon as he heard the name, I had him write it phonetically on a piece of paper. I handed it to the runner and sent it outside for one of my lieutenants to call in to headquarters. After I gave the intelligence guys what I thought was enough time to research his name, I stood up. Some of the senior police looked nervous, because any time I got up to go outside, it meant I was angry. I walked out into the cool night, breathing in the smells of heated sewage in the gutters. As soon as I stepped out onto the curb of the police station, two of my sergeants appeared to brief me on the situation.

"Sir, the local drunk is back and we took a grenade off of him tonight."

"Well, did you arrest him?" I asked with a look of expectation.

"No, sir, he's the uncle of one of the police lieutenants. We walked him back home."

"You see him again, arrest him," I demanded.

Turning from my NCOs, tired of these incidents, I got on my radio and asked for an update from intelligence. Although the man was on a blacklist, there was not much more information on him. Most of the names were connected to a terrorist group or act, but this guy was simply logged as a possible terrorist. I wasn't even sure how strongly we could trust the list. We'd been having a problem: Some of the folks arrested and detained turned out to be innocent and were usually snitched on by an informant who was at odds with the other person's tribe. Our intelligence people had a hard time figuring out who was lying and who was telling the truth. But I was trying to create working relationships with anyone connected to the city, on the list or not. As long as they weren't wanted for war crimes, I would check them out.

As a commander, I found myself thinking about these things often, and I had lots of opportunities to build relationships. I decided to make it pretty easy for this guy; the plan was to walk with him on patrol and kill him if anything bad or violent happened to me or my soldiers while we were out.

I went to him before the patrol, and said through my translator, "It is an honor for you to want to help me today. I would be privileged to have you walk by my side as we conduct this often-dangerous mission. But if we are attacked, this will be your last day of life."

I knew my translator got to the meat of the message because the cleric's eyes opened wide and he looked into mine.

I smiled and said, "Do you understand?"

He did. He responded, "Give me thirty minutes" and raced off in his car.

I knew I was taking a chance, for this was the night Doc warned me about the price on my head, but it seemed a chance worth taking. It was never unnerving, only frustrating. I had done so much to provide safety to the people of Hit. Now someone wanted to kill me and had put a price on my head? I was pissed.

I sent the cleric on ahead of us and honored his thirty minutes. Dressed in robes and a prayer cap, he scurried around the city, checking on his guards and ordering bad characters home (often drunk men with weapons threatening to kill Americans). After he returned, he joined me and we had our most quiet night yet. He dispersed crowds effortlessly and left little for us to do. It was an easy night and actually a nice stroll through the city. In our conversation, I learned a lot from the man. Stopping once for a rest, we shared some watermelon. It had never tasted so good.

My mission inside the city went well, but things at the edge of town were starting to heat up. My QRF got into position by midnight, conducted our patrol, and aside from smoking a few insurgents, found it to be a slow night. We also established another dismounted observation post to watch over a school where gunshots had been reported the last two nights. Although my men saw the shots, they could not pinpoint the enemy. We had to return fire at fire flashes from rifle muzzles. These snipers were well hidden, but we silenced them. Otherwise it was a quiet night. In the month since I had killed my first man, my attitude about death in war had definitely changed. Killing only a few men had become a quiet night. Reality had set in.

On 12 May, we were expecting another easy day. I'd gone to the police station early to begin assigning weapons and posts (we did not allow new police officers to take our weapons with them off duty). Then a man came in and warned the police about an out-of-town cleric who was meeting in the mosque and was encouraging people to attack coalition forces. When the man said the cleric's name, my intelligence sergeant perked his eyes and gave me a knowing look. By coincidence, the cleric who had been helping us, whom we had nicknamed Charlie, showed up. He said he would order the troublemaker out of the mosque so that we could arrest him. It looked like our mission was about to take a drastic change. But Charlie went to the mosque and returned half an hour later to tell us that the man had left town. I didn't trust his report; I was worried we were getting set up for an ambush. So I decided to proceed with the mission and head out.

My intelligence sergeant was ready to arrest Charlie, but I now felt that Charlie was my friend.

A little background here on clerics under the Hussein regime: Saddam was a Sunni Muslim. He empowered some Sunni clerics as his lieutenants to run their tribes and communities. They had control over police, security forces, and local militias; they were local "bosses."

After Saddam's fall and the end of his political machine, the Ba'ath Party, Charlie had stepped into the power vacuum. He proclaimed himself the leader of local security forces. He grew even more powerful: His control over the local forces also gave him control of the city's legitimate market, its black market, money exchange, credit, and patronage. Merchants in town depended on him to protect their shops from looters at night.

Despite his shady background, I made a choice to work with him rather than arrest him. In my judgment, the city would shut down if we brought him in; he was the only thing holding it together. I felt Charlie could only help me, because we had the same mission—to provide for the safety and security of the town. I gave Charlie's men permits for their weapons, with photographs and credentials. It was a risk, but I trusted him and I needed him. He secured the market, and the market was a dangerous place for us to be. He worked with me because we had a common goal. Our arrangement also saved lives— his men stopped shooting at us, so we didn't have to kill them. I even had Charlie escort me on some of the more dangerous missions.

After Charlie left the police station that night and we prepared to head back to camp, a grenade went off about two hundred meters away. A second one exploded another a hundred meters out. It was looking like it was going to be a fucked-up night, and I wanted Charlie's ass. It was obvious he wasn't in total control or that he had lost control. He was either going to work for me or find himself detained.

But despite the rough start, the patrol went fine, with not a single problem. Charlie seemed to have taken care of the so-called "Sons of Saddam." He stopped by during our patrol to show me the mosque they operated from. We marked it on the map, reported it to the operations center, and checked it out. The mosque appeared quiet and empty, so we continued to march. Then, back at the police station, we started collecting weapons back from the police. I sat as I normally did, with the chief, smoking cigarettes and trying to hydrate after five to ten miles of foot patrolling.

The chief and his lieutenants would always laugh at me for going on the patrols. They told me that it was the work of the "lower men."

To which I responded, "The families of those men out there have entrusted me with their lives and expect me to bring them home. I lead from the front. I am an American."

The chief responded, "Yes, but you cannot command your soldiers if you are killed. It is too dangerous on those streets."

I thought of the irony of a police chief telling me not to go out into his own streets because they were too dangerous. I laughed and said, "You have lots to learn, my friend."

■   ■   ■

Despite the occasional chaos, we were the model city in the Sunni triangle. We had skirmishes a few times a week, but most of the time, the place was relatively calm. People were getting on with their lives. One afternoon, the Army sent a team of reporters from the Army News Service to write a story about our progress. Besides quickly installing a mayor and police force, we were also making strides on improving the local infrastructure. It was not something you read very much about in the papers back home.

Just days after we arrived, the squadron acquired replacement generators and power for the local water treatment plant. It had been shut down for years, forcing people to drink the water out of the

Euphrates, which was polluted. The water looks like the stuff you see in theme park pools; thanks to chemicals and waste, it is an aqua blue. So you can imagine how pleased the people of Hit were when clean, fresh water poured out of their taps.

We brought people back to work at the phone company. They got existing phone lines back up and then wired civilian homes for service for the first time ever. We had to guard the work crews because they were often robbed for their copper parts. Army engineers also rebuilt the power grid, giving the city steady electricity twenty-four hours a day. We appointed the first woman director of power and telephone service. We secured the bank. We found the local banker, who had been in hiding, and convinced him to reopen the building. We opened the large bank vault; it was empty. Over the next weeks, we put money there that we found on patrols and raids. We'd discover trunks full of dinars bundled in bags when we pulled over suspects in their cars. Much of it had been stolen by Ba'ath Party officials. They didn't have any place else to hide it. In houses, we'd find bundles of dinars in mattresses, refrigerators, walls, grain sacks. Once it was back in the bank, we were able to start paying salaries to local government and utility workers, and the people of Hit were able to repay their debts and pay for goods with cash.

We filled gas tanks at the two gas stations in town with fuel supplied by U.S. contractors. We stood guard at the stations as drivers filled their cars; they paid ten cents a gallon. Sometimes we gave it away for free, if people had no money to purchase it. Policing fuel was a difficult task. Our focus was to get the fuel trucks to the gas stations safely and guard them until the underground tanks were filled. But some trucks never made it to the station—they were sometimes hijacked. The hijackers would then sell the gasoline on the black market.

My best memory from our rebuilding efforts was opening schools for children. With the new security, people felt safe enough to send their children back to school. For the first time, girls got to attend. Unfortunately, we had to fire and replace all the teachers, as they were usually high-ranking Ba'ath Party officials. The new school books offered students a real education, rather than propaganda. The kids would wave at us on their way to school. It felt good.

I was proud to be an American on foreign soil providing freedom. It was fulfilling to be able to see its effect on people and the way they lived. It was a city of success, and I can testify that we were making progress. With the exception of the former military and Ba'ath Party organizations, people in Iraq were getting back to living life.

■ ■ ■

Unfortunately, I believe that our fame as the model city was what brought the undesirables to town. It may have seemed an easy target to some, and in a way, it was. As a former Ba'ath Party leadership town, most lived off their Ba'ath Party welfare and sat around smoking cigarettes and arguing. There was a great opportunity to recruit and train terrorists, especially from among the youth, to interrupt our progress in town. We began to see more of it. We even caught children trying to throw grenades at us. Our intelligence was reporting more young people meeting in mosques to plan attacks on U.S. soldiers. We started to come across more handmade explosive devices and booby traps and raided weapons laboratories in homes. Even with all our successes behind us, a dark shadow of terrorism was starting to fall over the city.

I went into Hit a few days after our last contact with the RPG-firing insurgents to announce that we were pulling out of the city. The leaders in town were happy. We also scheduled some training required by V Corps. I was now tasked to train my new police force. The mayor asked for a week to regroup the force, and I was thankful for that. I needed time to establish a police academy.

Fortunately, our mounted operations were coming to a temporary halt in order to allow us to prepare for the police academy training. Patrols would resume after the one-week training workshop was complete. The only good part of this schedule was that the days went by quickly. With the burden of fatigue, and the new price on my head, I sure missed home.

■　■　■

As I prepared to move out on the next mission, I picked up the picture of Kim. Her words echoed from the frame: "I love you. I am thinking about you, and I hope you are kicking some royal Baghdad ass!"

As I kissed her image, I thought about our unborn child. It would still be a year before I met my son or daughter. But I prayed for its health.

"Lord, give me the strength to get through another mission in Iraq. Bless me with knowledge to outsmart my enemy, and give me the decisiveness that I will require to keep my soldiers alive. Help me bring them home safe. Bless my family, as they worry and pray for me now and always. Amen."

■   ■   ■

It was 1650 hours on 21 June. I was in my vehicle on my way to the soccer field. I felt confident, but was not at all excited about training green recruits. I thought back to my earlier concern about our route and decided to cut over on a dirt road to enter the stadium from behind. I hoped to get set before crowds formed around the perimeter. It was not a route I had briefed my men about, but it was a road we'd driven many times. It seemed like a good decision; there wouldn't be anyone on a dirt road to throw obstacles in our way. We'd also checked the road for mines when we'd first arrived in the area and hadn't found any. Nor did we have any new intelligence that mines had been placed on the road. I decided to take that route. A security team would go back down to the police station to get the officers moving to the training site.

Just as we came to the end of the road, I noticed the disturbed soil on the bank sloping down in front of my truck. I stopped the convoy. It looked a little different, a little steeper, unusual, but not dangerous—farmers were often at the site and would move dirt around all the time. I commanded the vehicle forward. A moment later, it hit the mine. More specifically, the right front tire activated it; it blew my truck off the ground, blinding me with smoke and dust. I wasn't sure exactly what had happened, but knew I was hurt.

Thank God for my flak jacket, because my chest plate was full of metal shards from the floorboards, engine, and metal wire from the radial tires. That's what I noticed first. Then I realized that my left foot was trapped between the frame and the sand. It was actually my left big toe that hurt the worst. Attempting to pull free, I put my right foot onto the ground, which was now at door level. That was the last time I ever used that foot. I pulled my left foot free. I turned and fell forward into First Sergeant Kabran's and Sergeant First Class McNichols's hands. As I tried to stand up, I looked down and saw my right foot collapsing under my weight, and blood and bone oozing out the side of my boot. Funny, in a way, considering I was so worried about my left foot. Shock, I suppose, kept me from realizing the truth of the matter.

Sergeant First Class McNichols and First Sergeant Kabran heroically carried me to the six-passenger truck designated as our medical evacuation truck, gathered up my driver, who had minor injuries, and hauled ass back to the base.

I gave my last order as Troop Commander, Killer 6, "Report the contact, secure the site, and evacuate the casualties."

Then, on a more personal note, I said to Sergeant First Class McNichols, "Get me the fuck out of here. I am fucked up. I need some treatment, hurry."

CHAPTER 9

In Her Own Words

by Kim Rozelle

WITH DAVID GONE, MY DAYS were filled with cross-stitching Beatrix Potter ABCs for the baby's room or shopping for material to finish the bed set for the nursery. That day, I planned to stitch until it was time to get ready for the baby shower my friends were throwing me that afternoon.

At about eight and a half months pregnant, I was waking up early in the morning. I was up that Saturday morning watching the news before the Saturday morning cartoons came on. I always liked having cartoons on the television on Saturday mornings. It distinguished the day from the weekdays to me.

It was about 8:30 AM when I heard the doorbell. I ran downstairs as quickly as one with a huge belly can run to find Carolyn Kievenaar, the squadron commander's wife, on the other side of the door. She wasn't at all who I expected, but I assumed it had something to do with a wife who was having some adjusting problems to the deployment.

She came inside and didn't hesitate: "Kim, there has been an accident."

My heart leapt to my throat. A rush of emotions welled up in me. I felt tears sting my eyes and forced them back so that I could focus on her next statement.

"David is okay."

I asked what happened and she insisted that we move to the den to talk. As we walked to the den, I was already feeling better because of the word "okay," trying to keep a level head for whatever bad news she was about to tell me.

She told me that she had gotten word from her husband that David had run over an anti-tank mine in his Humvee and had injured his foot. The initial word was "no loss of life or limb." I felt a sense of full relief wash over me. My thought was, "Okay, David will come home, have surgery, do a few months of physical therapy, and then return to his command in Iraq." Like others already had.

I knew he would get over damage to a foot, but to lose his command prematurely and leave his men to someone else would be a hard hit for him.

Since I have known David, who was a lieutenant when we met, he has been one of the most patriotic people I have ever known. He is not too military, such that it's all he talks about, but when he does, he is very serious about it. He always enjoyed his time out in the field and the experiences he had with his soldiers. He tried to take it all in: the soldiers, his peers, and his superiors, to see how to best meet all their needs. He looked forward to using those observations in his command as a captain. Just as any armored captain would, he went to many training stations to prepare for his command, either in the field or as a staff officer. Once he became a commander, he was elated to see his training and the training he gave to his soldiers paying off. His goal was to do the best for all his men and to see his command through any hard times, whatever they might be. My knowing how much energy he put into his command was what made me worry about his losing it.

So Carolyn and I sat there and talked while we waited for further word about David's situation and injury status. We talked about events that concerned us as Family Readiness Group leaders and as military wives. A subject of concern was how David was not the first commander or officer to be injured since the 3rd ACR had been there. I told her how I had let myself believe that as an officer, he might not be as much in harm's way. That proved to not be true; David confessed later how many times he had felt bullets zip just past him.

Carolyn kept looking at her phone and finally called home to ask her daughter if her husband had called and to not say anything if anyone should call with questions about David.

I was starting to feel comfortable again, as if she were there only on a friendly visit—instead of it being early in the morning, me still in my maternity pajamas, learning of David's injury. However, I kept having a nagging thought: "Why is she still here?" If the reports were that things were minor, there may not be much word for a while. At least long enough for her to encourage me to get dressed, eat some breakfast, and move on with the day. Instead, we were just sitting there trying to talk about the familiar while she had a death grip on her cell phone. The situation was starting to bug me. Then, the unfortunate answer to that question came.

Her cell phone rang. I knew it was her husband. But I swallowed my heart back down into my gut again as I saw her hold her head with her hand and look down, away from me.

I thought, "This can't be good." I didn't know quite what she would say when she stopped uttering the somber "uh-huhs" and "okays."

Once again, she didn't mince words when she got off the phone. She hit the "end" button on her phone, looked up at me, and said, "They had to amputate. He lost his right foot."

I can't fully describe how I felt. Maybe a steel-toed boot kick in my baby-filled stomach while fifty knives were being stabbed into my whole body might do it. I soon lost all control of myself as I have never, ever before. I heard myself wailing, "Oh, David. Oh, David." I heard screams and realized they were coming from me.

My thoughts and emotions were of how David must be feeling. I imagined him looking down to see no foot. I was horrified. I had not even thought that this might happen. How much pain was he in? He must be so confused. My last thought I allowed myself of his pain was, "I hope his spirit is not broken." I knew then that my previous hopes of his returning to his command had to be abandoned.

I almost didn't realize it, but Carolyn was trying to hug me to comfort me. There I was, with this huge belly, still in my pajamas, with the SCO's wife trying to wrap her arms around me. I felt repulsed. I didn't want hers or anyone else's comfort at that moment. Not while David had to be so miserable.

I think I started to push her away as I tried to gain control of myself. I started saying, "I feel the numbness coming." I said it as truth as much as a way to nicely say, "Get off me."

I am not typically a real hugs-and-kisses person to start with. I usually mess up hugs or kisses even with David. That used to be how we would start a long-awaited visit together, with bruised, bloody noses from the attempt at a dramatic kiss at the airport.

Carolyn pulled back and I just sat there with the hiccups you get after a big cry.

After a while, we started talking about the information she was given since the initial word. We both found it odd that he went from "no loss of life or limb" to an amputation. We had obviously been misinformed. Then our thoughts went to the anti-tank mine that had done the deed. How did he survive an anti-tank mine in a Humvee? And why had we not gotten word of anyone else hurt as seriously? Not that we wanted to hear of more injuries, but it just didn't measure up.

I wanted to know if David had been a part of the decision to amputate or if the decision had been made for him. I couldn't help but think back to the beginning of the movie *Dances with Wolves*: Kevin Costner's character, John Dunbar, wakes up in a medical tent to see a table piled with shattered limbs cut from soldiers' bodies. Had he not found the strength to get up off that table, his leg would have been on top of that mound.

I wanted to talk to David but thought it would be a while. He was just going into surgery when I got the news and needed a cell phone to make a call.

The reality that David's parents needed to be notified started becoming painfully clear to me. Although I really was numb, I would quietly cry every few minutes as another bad thought would cross my mind, either for the first time or as a nasty repeated, unanswered thought. I told Carolyn I wanted to try to tell them myself. I felt I owed them that. However, if I couldn't follow through, she should be ready to take over.

In thinking of whom to call, I knew that David's father, John, would be the more stable recipient. I really didn't even want to talk to his mother, Judy, or sister, Amy, because I thought they would break down on me and I couldn't handle that right then. I assumed they were the type who would try to make me feel better with words of "comfort" when they themselves were nowhere near comfortable enough to not put their woes on me. I was nobody's rock that morning, as I was barely my own. After all my anticipation, they surprised me later that day.

To change the scenery and to ensure better reception and a clear call, we moved to the back patio to call John. He answered. I still regret what I said, and therefore did, to him. All I got out was, "John, David has been in an accident." And I started sobbing. It was the first time I had tried to tell the story since hearing it myself, one that even I had yet to truly believe had happened. How horrified he must have been to hear those words over the phone from his daughter-in-law about his only son. His mind must have taken him to a terrible place for that instant before Carolyn took over. I had done exactly what I didn't want to happen to me. Carolyn had made sure I didn't have the worst possible experience, and yet, I put that on David's father. I hope he can forgive me.

I practically threw the phone at Carolyn and was left sitting there sobbing again with the rush of my own emotions mixed with regret over failing to be strong for John. I have always wanted to ask his forgiveness for informing him that way but find it hard to revisit that moment.

Carolyn took the phone and walked across the yard to talk to John, away from my loud sobs. In the meantime, the rear detachment commander, also my neighbor, came over, and I could tell he was relieved to see Carolyn there. That meant that he didn't have to do what she had already done. She finished talking to John and told me that he said he would tell the rest of the family. That was what I had hoped he would say. I knew he would come through. I felt great respect for him then. I felt remorse for not having the strength to tell him myself and not talking personally to him about a plan of action.

I don't know exactly what he and Carolyn talked about, his reactions then, or how he felt when he got off the phone. I also only know bits and pieces of what it was like for David's family that day.

The regimental commander's wife, Susan Teeples, came as well, which made me feel good that she would make the time. She reassured me that David would be taken care of and that he would be offered the regimental headquarters command in spring 2004. I asked her about my concerns of David's participation in the decision to amputate. She assured me that they would do nothing without his consent. She also told me that her neighbor, a colonel in the medical field, was most likely there, or was the one to perform the initial amputation. She talked about how good, thorough, professional, and nice a man he was. It made me feel a little better to hear that if David chose to and was able to, he would be taken care of in his career that he loved, and that he had been taken care of medically already.

I couldn't help feeling sorry for these two ladies charged to sit there and tell me these things no one wants to hear. This was only an injury. How bad it must be to inform someone of a death.

K Troop had been lucky so far. There had been no serious injuries or deaths. So I, as the FRG leader, did not have to do what Carolyn and Sue were doing for me. I'm not sure I would do as well in relaying information. They were my rocks. Not too many hugs or sappy support, but they figured out what I needed and gave me only that.

Just before Sue left, David's mother called. As soon as I heard her voice, I tensed up, expecting the worst. But she did very well—she only cried a little. She called to say that she knew and that she was there for me if I needed her. Amy said the same when she called later.

I had no family members nearby. Although they all offered to come, I turned them down. I didn't want everybody staring at me, waiting for me to break down. I would have gone home if it were possible. But I was too far in the pregnancy to fly or start over with a new doctor and hospital. And I knew my mother was arriving on 22 July to help me with the birth and the baby.

My father surprised me. He told me how much he thought of David as a man, provider, husband, and person. My father doesn't give out compliments often or lightly. I could tell the news really upset him. My mother was wonderful, as usual, and quite supportive and a great listener. She was another rock for me, but admitted later that she called her sisters after talking to me and broke down.

My family has loved David like another son since the day they met him. We like to joke about how much he charmed them—and duped them. I say duped only because he was so polite then and is such a jokester now. My father was a noncommissioned officer in the Forced Recon Marines in the Vietnam War. He won't talk about it with me but talks readily to David, which is partly because David understands the talk better than I do. I think David's injury reminded my dad of some of the things he experienced in his war.

■　■　■

Carolyn kept telling me I didn't have to go to the baby shower planned for that afternoon, but that if I did go, she would go with me. She had been so good all day, being honest with me and not smothering me. I decided to go to the shower. The only problem was making sure no one there knew or found out what had happened. I didn't want my baby shower to turn into a sob-fest filled with, "We are so sorry," "What can we do?" "How do you feel?" Having Carolyn go with me might bring up questions because it was not usual at the time for us to be together. Not that we weren't friends, just not as close as we soon would be.

My other worry was that I might miss a call from David. However, we assumed he would still be under from the surgery and probably wouldn't even try to call until the next day. I also knew that the ladies had put so much into throwing this shower for me. I didn't want to let them down. Plus, my heart and mind could use a break from the somber situation that sitting in my den had turned out to be.

Just as I was going upstairs to shower before the party, David called. I assumed it was more family calling, and when I heard his weak voice on the other end, I had to ask if it was really him. He started talking and was trying to tell me he was in an accident when I interrupted and told him to stop because I already knew. I didn't want him going through the agony of trying to tell me himself. I said a quick "thank you" to Carolyn in my head for telling me the news earlier. By now, the shock had worn off. I can't imagine how horrible it would have been if David was the one to tell me for the first time.

He asked how I knew and I quickly told him about Carolyn's visit. I heard the confusion in his voice turn to relief when he understood that he didn't have to tell me the news himself.

I ran outside and sat on the edge of the patio to get better reception and privacy. There was also something uplifting about having the sun and sky over me instead of the dark house, kept dark with closed blinds and curtains to keep the heat down in the record Colorado summer we were having. Being out there made me feel more connected with David.

I don't recall the exact conversation. David remembers even less of it; he was so drugged up. It was only a few hours after the amputation. I do remember that he joked about at least losing his bad foot: His right foot had been broken and sprained a few times while the left foot had not. I felt better at hearing him joke about that.

Then, I don't know if it was the drugs or what, but his next comment rocked my world and scared me more than I had been thus far.

He said, "I think I've given enough." And then he started crying.

I knew what he meant. I told him to stop right there because no decisions either way would be made until he was home and we could talk about all the options. We both knew already of the incentives the colonel was offering, but we had a lot to consider and a lot we didn't know about yet.

His comment scared me partly because we had planned on staying in the Army for the full twenty years. We agreed that we would take stock of the situation every so often, when most people do, just before promotions or station changes. If we were absolutely miserable, then we would get out. But the plan was to stay in so he could retire at about forty-two and start a new career with the military retirement salary and the remaining medical benefits to act as an anchor for our finances. We thought it was the smart thing to do, seeing how volatile the civilian world could be with jobs and benefits. Most older retirees we talked to had done the same. They were glad to have that money coming in every month to support them through good times and bad.

When David asked how I was doing, I told him I was fine. I knew he was worried about me and the baby. I told him what a great friend Carolyn was being to me and that she would be going to the shower with me. I asked him if it was crass of me to go and he agreed that it was not.

He finally said he had to go rest, if he could, because the pain and confusion was a lot to bear. I didn't protest because I could tell his mind was wandering. I told him how much I loved him and how I wished I could be there, and said goodbye as I choked back the swelling sobs.

The ironic thing about David's call was how clear it was. In the time he had been gone, the calls were few and very short. Not much was actually said in those calls due to the static and echo and the delay caused us to talk over one another. He usually called in the middle of the night, around two in the morning for me. I asked him to do so in order to be sure I was home and not out running errands. To come home from the grocery store to see that you missed a call from your deployed husband is devastating. Our conversations consisted of the same things, statements of our love for each other, asking if we are each okay, and his asking about things at home. Not much more was said since I was not allowed to ask questions about what he was doing or where he was in Iraq. We had had a whole security briefing on it before he left. So, when his family found out he had called, they would search me for information, and I usually had none. I know it disappointed them, but calls were hard to come by out there and expensive. He usually had to wait in line for an average of four hours to get to a phone in the hopes the connection would actually go through.

I filled Carolyn in on the call from David, omitting his comment about having given enough. I wanted to keep things light and to admit that would have brought us both down. I went upstairs to take a shower. I moved between dumb shock and sobbing, with the warm water flowing over my swollen body. I looked down at my huge stomach and wondered how all this would affect the little person in there. I didn't want to dwell on it. I knew stress would not be good for the baby and that was exactly what everyone was worried about. I got out and put on one of the nice linen maternity outfits Judy had bought me. I almost felt like all was normal.

Carolyn and I showed up at the shower and greeted everyone there. I was excited to see all the ladies who were involved. They were ladies in K Troop and friends I had made since moving to Colorado. Karen Chumbley and Shannon Richkowski were the two who set the thing up and did a great job. As the games were played, food and cake was eaten, and finally, gifts were opened, I kept repeating to myself, "I am sitting here laughing while my husband has no foot. . . . I am sitting here laughing and having fun while my husband lies there in pain without a foot."

Those thoughts haunted me throughout the shower, no matter how hard I tried to push it all aside and enjoy the party the ladies were trying to give me. I had to push reality aside for fear that the sobs would return. That was the last thing I wanted to happen, to break down in front of those ladies. While I did have bad thoughts, I did well living in the moment. I almost didn't want the shower to end. At the party's end, I asked Karen and Shannon to come by my house to help with the gifts and told them I had something to talk to them about. I put it as lightly as I could.

Once inside, with all the gifts brought in, I awkwardly started telling the two women about David, with Carolyn standing nearby.

"The reason I asked the two of you here is that I have good news and bad news. I wanted you to hear it from me first, since you two are so important to me."

I hesitated a second, took a breath, and said, "David is coming home!"

They both looked confused by my statement. So I continued, "That is the good news. The bad news is why he is coming home." This next part I rushed through so I could get it out before the sobs made it incoherent. "He was injured by a mine and they had to amputate his foot."

They both put their hands to their faces and looked back at me with shock. Then the tears started. They both took it hard, but I do believe that Shannon took it harder. Her husband is named David as well. Our two Davids are great friends, but are different men. Hers stands at about 5'7", while mine is a good six feet. So we came to call the two good friends Little Dave and Big Dave. Although they officially met in Korea in 2000, they had actually followed much the same route in the Army, Big Dave being a little ahead. After working with Little Dave and being very impressed with him, Big Dave pulled some strings and pushed for Little Dave to move right into the 3rd ACR and, essentially, right into command as soon as he arrived at Fort Carson. My Dave had done some staff time before getting his command, but Little Dave moved right into command because of Big Dave's efforts. This and other events made it seem as if Big Dave was taking care of Little Dave. Not that Little Dave couldn't hold his own, but it always helps to have someone give a little push for you, especially as a peer.

Taking care of Little Dave was how Shannon thought of things in Iraq. It made her feel better that her husband had someone looking out for him. David admitted later that he was indeed looking out for his buddy, who did not have the same training as he did in urban operations. On a few occasions, my Dave had asked for some potentially dangerous missions to be given to him instead of to Dave Richkowski. Little Dave knew what was going on and didn't exactly like it. After my

Dave left, Little Dave was working in a different region and got to do some of those missions after all, and did quite well.

So when I told Shannon that the guy she thought was looking out for her husband—even if it was really just as a friend to talk to out there—was coming home without a foot blew her away. I put on a brave face for her and told her my Dave would be fine one way or another and that hers would do fine as well in Iraq without my husband. He was a big boy and didn't need a guard.

A point to be made about the two Daves' friendship is that the SCO issued a special order: No one was to tell Dave Richkowski about what happened to my Dave until Butch told him himself. So, as soon as possible, Butch flew to Little Dave's location and told him. I heard he took it hard but handled it well.

Hearing the truth from the SCO was much better than for him to hear the rumors that my Dave had been killed, which was the rumor that had traveled to the regimental headquarters (RHHT). My David found that out later from a friend in RHHT, who admitted that he had cried a river before finding out it wasn't true.

After telling the two women about all the details I knew and letting them cry and ask if I needed anything, I encouraged them on their way. I had already had a long day.

Karen had been dealing with enough on her own front. Her own health was in jeopardy—she had cancer—and that news was like a roller coaster. She had already been living one week in hope and the next in doubt. Her husband, Phillip, was David's first sergeant, and she had become a good friend of mine since David had taken command.

I told her we would be fine and that I would definitely let her know if I needed anything. Karen can tend to put others before herself too much, so I definitely did not want to put any more on her. I put on an even braver face for her.

The two ladies left after a while and I turned to Carolyn, still sitting there. I told her I was fine and needed to get to bed soon. She offered to rush over if I needed anything.

She left and I sat back into the wingback chair I had been sitting in when I was in the den during the day. It was the chair I had made my own when arranging the house. Mostly I preferred it since I had the lamp positioned over the chair for better light while cross-stitching and the ottoman in front to prop my feet on. Each house we move into has a different configuration for our furniture, depending on the space. So each new location presented a different "favorite spot." That wingback chair had become not only my favorite spot, but also was my comfort during that time.

Soon after Carolyn left, David called again. I was really surprised, as it was morning already for him in his part of the world. His injury occurred in the morning for me, but it was night for him then. This time he sounded a little more coherent. I asked him a few questions that had been bothering me. First, I was concerned about his role in the decision to amputate. He said he made that decision. I felt a load lift off my shoulders at that comment. Then I asked how he had even survived an anti-tank mine in just a Humvee. He told me how the enemy would lay some anti-tank mines upside down to be sure they detonated at all. Set upright, a mine has a small trigger area. The explosion can tear a hole through a tank. Set upside down, as this one was, it explodes with less concentration outward, but more force directly up. That lucky break, and the fact that he was at the edge of the mine when it exploded, resulted in less injury. He also found out what kind of mine it was, and that there were at least ten other mines lying around the field, waiting for him and his men.

Things started to make sense to me. With the confusion cleared up, I could look at the whole situation. It allowed me to picture the scene in my head in place of the surreal imaginings of before.

We talked about how we wished we could be together and how the baby was doing. I knew that the Army would send me straight to Germany to be at his side if I were not so far along with the baby. I hated the situation. Although it was looking as though there was a chance he could make it home for the birth of the baby after all, I would have to bite my nails until he was home. He would have to be alone or with others more able to sit by his bedside. I have never felt so far away from him as we finally hung up after saying how much we loved each other.

It was still light outside, for it was still afternoon. I realized, again, how nice the day had been besides the heat. The day had gone by so fast. I reflected that it must have been how the families in New York City felt on September 11, as they got word of injured or lost family and friends. A perfectly good day blurred by such tragedy. It was partly because of that perfect, yet, blurry day that my husband had been in Iraq to have his foot blown off.

I remember September 11 just as most people do: what they were doing when they found out and how that day will stay in their memories. It is the "day Kennedy was shot" for my generation.

But not everyone feels that way about September 11. My favorite memory of how naïve some folks were, even after the attacks in New York and the Pentagon, was one David tells about how he sat there in line trying to get back on post. As he sat listening to constant updates on the radio stations, a civilian stopped his truck, rolled down the window, and asked David what was going on.

The man asked, "What's the hold-up?"

David said, "The World Trade Center, man."

The guy asked, "What does that have to do with anything?"

David didn't respond; he just looked at him with a dumb look, as he should have, and rolled the window back up.

September 11 was a long day for America. But I had David there with me, and close friends to talk to about things that had happened to others two thousand miles away. This day, June 21, I had come a long way from watching cartoons in order to distinguish the day from a weekday. That day was distinguished from any other day of the week by being without my husband, and worrying about bad things that had happened to him, not someone else, anywhere else. I was exhausted.

■   ■   ■

A few days later, I decided it was time to give the news about David to friends. I sent out an e-mail telling them the basics and that I and his family would appreciate it if any responses were by letter or e-mail as we didn't want to be bombarded by calls. The response was astounding. We received messages from friends and co-workers we had not heard from in ages. I guess the word traveled fast. Old college buddies, high school coaches, friends who had gotten out of the Army also sent word of their concern. I thought it was great! I printed out the stacks of emails and couldn't wait to show David. Most messages expressed the same thought—that they knew if anyone could get through this, David could. I prepared the printed emails, letters, and cards as a presentation to David when he got home. I knew there would come a time that he would need the pick-me-up.

I began to get more nervous about his arrival home. David was being transferred from Baghdad to Germany, and from there to Walter Reed Medical Center in Washington, D.C.

I was not sure what he might need for his physical state. We lived in a two-story house and I knew that the stairs would be a challenge. I knew he had already learned how to maneuver them with his crutches at the hospital, but there were not as many there as we had in this house. I wasn't sure how things would work out; I just knew I wanted him home. Every day he was away, so close as "in country," was another day closer to the baby arriving and him missing it by a few states instead of by another part of the world.

■ ■ ■

A month later, the time had come for David to finally come home. He had gotten a last-minute flight one day earlier than expected. So I called Carolyn and Karen Chumbley to let them know and to see if they wanted to join me in greeting him at the airport. They jumped on the offer.

I made sure the house was clean, ran to the store to get anything he could want to have, and got myself dressed in my late-term maternity clothes. I grabbed the banner I had made with Shannon Richkowski and ran by the store to get a balloon and some flowers for his welcome home. Carolyn came by to pick me up. I was nervous.

We sat in the café seats just outside the security area. Since it was harder for me to get up and down, Carolyn did all the hopping from her seat to look down the walkway for any signs of David. Finally she said she could see him.

I was pretty calm up until that point. A little nervousness turned into feelings of nausea. I wanted so badly to put on a brave face for him but wasn't sure I could do it. I hadn't seen him in over three months. The few emailed pictures of him in Iraq were the only frame of reference I had for how he would look at the end of the walkway. He had warned me he would not look good and to be prepared for a shock.

I had pictured a lot worse than what I saw, but the shock of seeing him again still took hold of me. His shrapnel wounds had mostly healed on his face and arms. He was so skinny—never a word I imagined using to describe David. He was always so fit and muscular. His face was sunken in; his hair had grown only a few millimeters since his last bald shaving. He was wearing clothes I had sent him while he was in Walter Reed. Packing that box was so different for me after packing the loaded care packages for him while in Iraq. This time, there were no wipes or hand sanitizer, but clothes he would wear around the house.

One leg was bent in the wheelchair foothold while the other was propped upright with his crutch. For the first time, I saw his stump.

The whole picture was such a shock that I started sobbing, as I stood there holding his balloon and flowers.

I think it upset him to see me explode into tears like that. He didn't want to scare me; it is not a good thing to have your wife bawl when she sees you for the first time since an injury. Any hope he may have had that he looked better was thrown out the window. What he was forgetting was that I had not seen the absolute worst to know that this was better.

We hugged and kissed and took a few pictures. Then I stepped aside to let Carolyn and Karen have their chance at him. We had all agreed to keep the welcome committee small and more personal. Too many people would have overwhelmed him, and me as well.

As we strolled him around the airport to the luggage area, people kept coming up to him and saying, "Thank you for your service." That meant so much to both of us. It really warmed my heart.

As we pulled up to the house, David saw the huge banner that hung in front of the garage. It said, "Welcome Home Big Daddy!" He loved it.

David was home. It was a little awkward at first. Both of us wanted things to be back to normal, but they obviously were not. A lot was not the way it used to be. He was home when he was supposed to be in Iraq. He also didn't have a foot and was in a lot of pain, and I was pregnant with a baby who would change our lives. We had a lot on our plate. But we held on to each other and took care of each other as best we could. I tried not to dwell on all the unanswered questions I had, because there were too many and they would be answered in time.

CHAPTER 10

Taking My Foot Does Not Mean Taking My Life

"AAAAGGH!" WAS ALL I COULD HEAR IN MY EAR. I thought, "Is that me screaming? No, it can't be, my mouth is too dry." Looking up, I found the eyes of Sergeant First Class McNichols, and he said, "Sir, it is going to be alright. Stay calm, I'm treating Westman for shock."

All I could say was, "Yes, treat him first, but . . . water."

I looked over and saw Westman with his uniform torn open, still screaming, and a face full of tears, with several people crouched over assessing injuries and pouring water on his chest and face. He was terrified. He had enough action already—it seemed that every day I looked at him, drew my weapon, and said, "Drive right into the middle of those people. Let's break that shit up." He thought of me as fearless, and had even put KOWBOY 6 on the windshield above my name.

He often asked me, "Sir, doesn't it scare you to run right into the middle of things? You are crazy."

The difference we found between us was that he would think about his wife at home and worry about his own safety, while I was thinking only of the safety of Iraq. My safety was secondary, and I was dependent on my men to protect me. I wasn't fearless, but I certainly was never scared. Even then, lying on my back, feeling the crushed bones in my feet and the blood pouring down my legs, arms, and neck, I was not afraid.

I looked up at Sergeant First Class McNichols, who was looking down at my leg with a concerned look. I said to him, "Elevate it . . . fuck, it's throbbing. Is Westman okay?"

Mac put a hand on my shoulder and said, "Yes. Sir, you are going to be alright."

I had taken the class on treating for shock a thousand times, and knew the routine: assess the casualty, reassure the casualty (if conscious), send immediate report of wounds, loosen restrictive clothing and elevate feet, move to a shaded area, provide first aid as you reassure the casualty, and evacuate to the next level of care. Mac was going through the steps, just as he had taught it so many times.

But between his reassurances, he would say, "Goddamn, sir." To make me laugh, he said it again, "Just a walk in the park, sir."

What was coming back to haunt me were all of the times I briefed an operations order in Iraq and ended my commander's comments with, "It's just a walk in the park, Killer."

Mac always had a way of getting me back. Not only had he warned me about our level of training in dismounted operations compared to infantry soldiers, but now he was treating me on an evacuation, after all the times he asked me not to lead the convoys. But he was there, as he always was, taking care of me.

Mac tore open my flak vest and pulled open my clothes. He poured the cool water on my chest, making me skip a breath and then breathe deeply again. I opened my mouth to beg like a baby bird, and took in a small drink. He looked at me funny because we both knew I wasn't supposed to have any water. One of the rules of treating shock is that you don't give water to a patient, but I was dying of thirst. Then it hit me. The hazy veil of shock was lifted.

Our method of treating shock works. Just as I swallowed, I felt the pain—as if someone had slammed my foot with a ten-pound sledgehammer. It was the delayed feeling of what it should have felt like during the blast. I leaned forward, gritted my teeth, and looked at my foot for the first time since my last step. My leg was straight and my foot was misshapen and slumped over to the right, lifeless. It wasn't just limp, but was grotesquely contorted at a severe angle well beyond ninety degrees. As I adjusted my leg, trying to find any sort of comfort, it turned around at even greater angles. Whenever I tried to move it, pain would run up my leg as if someone were shooting me in the foot again and again. The only thing holding my foot onto my body was my boot. The blood was now pouring down the inside of the cargo wall. It was thick and dark, and carried fragments of bone and tissue with it.

As we bumped down the road, I yelled at the driver, "Drive fast, but avoid the bumps!" Each time we would hit even the tiniest pebble in the road, my foot would bounce off the cargo seat and jiggle back into a resting position. As it did, I could feel every broken bone rubbing against each other, like rolling dry hay in your hand. I could feel the crunching deep in my soul, and reached back for something to firmly hold. I screamed, "Is this the fucking bumpiest road in Iraq?"

Lying flat in the back of the cargo Humvee, with my foot up on a troop seat, we raced north along the highway. The road was nothing but constant bumps, with craters and sections of mismatched concrete. Additionally, our Humvees are not known for a smooth ride, and the truck was jolting at every bump. All I could find to hold was the flap of an empty MRE box. The cardboard was perfect to tug on. The all-weather cardboard was hard to tear and bend and allowed me to hold and squeeze. For brief moments, I forgot about my legs.

The trip back was only about five minutes, but the pain was unbearable. As we pulled into camp, I imagined what my men must be thinking and doing. I worried about being litter-carried in front of my men. I did not want them to see me like that. Fuck, they never even saw me sleep, and now they would see me carried in like the dead.

My medics, who had not gone on the mission with me, waited on me at the front gate. Jon Kluck was the first man I saw as I was lifted out of the vehicle. He was angry.

Once I got to the main aid station, they cut off all my clothes and my boots. I lay naked and outstretched. The surgeon, also known as Doc, quickly identified the main injury, but made me aware of others around my body. The shrapnel in my face was treated at the same time as they inspected my feet. Fortunately, my left foot had only suffered some trauma.

As they cut off my right boot, they were simultaneously sticking me with IVs in both arms. I was more worried about my foot, but certainly noticed the sting of each needle as it poked into my veins. As they cut the boot, I could feel the discomfort of my dangling foot, now free. They were trying to support it, but there was no way to make it comfortable. The feeling of my boot coming off was a definite release of weight, but it also invited new pain.

Without X-rays, Doc was not able to make a good assessment and said I probably wouldn't lose my foot, which was the message that went to the higher command and home to Kim.

I remember looking down at the foot that they were now unsuccessfully trying to splint and thinking, "How can you save that?"

As it was peeled back, like meat filleted from the bone, I was not sure if I could trust his promise. To calm me down, they had to give me some oxygen. They kept telling me to calm down, but I couldn't slow my breathing. Besides the two IVs, they gave me one pop of morphine in the leg, which was not near enough. I wished that I were unconscious.

I reached my hand out to my XO, but he didn't understand what I needed. My tears were blinding me now, and I reached for a medic who was trying to tape off the surgical tubing that was running to my IV bags. I grabbed his hand, and he first withdrew, back to his work. I looked at him and squeezed, and he stopped and squeezed back. I just needed someone to hold my hand.

I looked over at the gallery of people who came to support me, but I could not acknowledge them. I was so angry. My command was over, and the war, for me, was over. I had lost everything in an instant.

And all I could say was, "Water."

Doc came back over and briefed me, "You need some serious attention, and the bird is on the way. We are going to transport you to the landing zone. Are you okay?"

Again, "Water."

Finally, one of the medics gave me a small sip, and I nodded that I was ready. Everyone wanted to grab hold of the litter, as though I were a celebrity. I had six guys trying to carry me through a door and then a turn. As I went out the door, they pinched my arm on the bare, broken cinderblock that was the doorway. I screamed in anger, and looked down to see fresh blood on my arm. Talk about adding insult to injury.

As I was loaded into the ambulance, Jon Kluck yelled out, "You'll be back by chow, sir."

I cut him as stern a look as I could, and said, "Yeah . . . sure."

Without saying it this time, I gave him what felt like a smile and a nod, which meant, for the first time since Kuwait, "You're in charge." He acknowledged with a salute, but looked sad and worried.

The helicopter finally arrived, but not nearly soon enough. I don't know why, but rather than landing at the marked landing zone, they took me out into the motor pool. As they pulled up in the ambulance and were ready to unload, I saw my row of tanks.

One of the medics yelled out to my men, "Can a couple of you guys help unload and load? He's heavy!"

I knew that the guys in the motor pool did not yet know about my injury. As soon as I heard footsteps running across the pavement, I worried what my men would think. I was embarrassed again.

I looked up to see the shocked face of one of my tank commanders, Staff Sergeant Jones, who said, "What the fuck are you doing there, sir? What happened?"

I looked up pitifully and said, "They got me."

■   ■   ■

Getting medically evacuated in a helicopter is no thrill ride. As soon as I was uncomfortably loaded, the crew chief, who looked like an astronaut with his giant helmet and darkened visor, briefed me on actions on contact and crash landing.

When he was done, he asked if I had any questions. I said, "Fuck you, you better not get shot down. You tell that pilot to fly like the devil."

He laughed and gave a "thumbs up" to the pilot. Once in flight, they gave me something to help with the pain, but it did little.

The crew chief had told me, "I just want to take the edge off."

I thought, "Fuck, man, my foot just got blown off. I need some pain medicine, now!" I yelled up at him, "I need more!"

With his helmet on and the sound of the aircraft drowning me out, he asked, "What?"

After playing the "yell and 'what?'" game, which is a normal conversation on a helicopter without a headset, I grabbed him by the shirt and said, "Give me more painkiller!"

But I had no luck. He just looked at me with his bee-like head and made wide shaking motions, and said, "Surgery... no way. I don't want to overmedicate."

I am not sure if he understood me or just ignored me, but the constantly bouncing aircraft was killing me, so I said, "I am going to throw you out of this helicopter if you don't give me some fucking pain medicine!"

He went back to work on me, and did give me something stronger. Before I knew it, we were landing. As the door to the helicopter opened again, the wind and sand distracted me from my pain.

From the time I hit the ground I was in motion. I was at a field hospital outside of Baghdad. They loaded me on a wheeled litter carrier and ran me into the operating room.

What I remember most about the hospital is a bunch of good-looking nurses asking the same questions over and over. "What's your name? How old are you? Do you know where you are? What unit are you in? Are you in pain?"

The last question killed me, and I would summon the energy to give them the look, which directly implied, "Yes, dumb ass, it hurts."

Each person asked the same questions again and again. I could put up with it from the hot nurses, but not when the dudes started asking. Especially when the orthopedic surgeon entered the room, and we went through the questions again. Added to that, they had me sign a bunch of releases. I actually had to laugh at that fact. I was injured in combat and had to sign a release to authorize surgery. It seemed unreal.

The doctor did a quick assessment of my foot and came to the head of my bed. I will always appreciate his straightforwardness and honesty. He explained that there was nothing left to save. The heel bone did not exist. Every other bone in my foot was crushed, and there was a nice hole through the center. There were also no tendons left attached anywhere in my foot. Whatever he put together would look like a clubfoot, and probably would never heal. If it did heal, I would not be able to be active on it. His words broke my heart.

He said, "I can save your foot, but you will probably have it cut off after a year or two of pain and frustration. Or, I can cut it off today, and you will be running on a prosthesis in a year."

I asked for a few minutes to lie back and cry.

I called the surgeon back and said, "Fuck it, take it!"

■ ■ ■

As they were prepping me for surgery, there were lots of people all around me. When I came to, there were only a few. They were the same beautiful nurses who had been asking me all the questions before, and were there to bring me back to life. Kim jokes with me about these "sirens," about them not being real, but rather part of some drug-induced fantasy, but it was true. I awoke to several beautiful ladies who were attending to me as I came off my medication. One was a psychiatrist who wanted to ensure I was going to handle the trauma okay. She stayed with me all night. Whenever I woke, she was there with a smile. It was nice, and I don't even know her name. All the ladies were that kind of pure sweetness. One even worked a second shift to take care of me. They did their job, because I had not even realized yet that my foot was really gone.

The best thing those ladies did was hand me a cell phone. As soon as I was lucid enough to know where I was, they asked me if I wanted a phone to call home. I had been trying to call home for weeks, and here I was having a phone handed to me. I was so excited. But I was also still very drugged, and barely remember calling Kim, and don't remember talking to my mother at all. I do remember when I was on with Kim that I was thrilled to hear her voice but then stunned at what I had to tell her.

I struggled for words, and said, "Kim...I've been injured...but I'm okay."

What a relief when she said, "I know, Carolyn is here and she told me everything."

I cried out loud, but kept the phone pressed to my ear, listening to what she knew.

Then she asked, "Were you conscious and did you get to choose to lose your foot?"

I explained to her how the decision had taken place, but then faded away, relieved at having notified my wife.

■　■　■

It was when I woke up again that it struck me. It actually takes several months for an amputee to actualize the loss of a limb, but I remember waking up and looking down at my elevated stump. It was swollen to the size of my head, and throbbed with pain. I felt so dirty, and my legs itched from the iodine. After a few minutes of staring at my injuries, I looked around, and found an Iraqi staring at me from an adjacent bed.

Just then, my nurse, Deann, walked into my section of the tent and said, "Good, you're awake."

I asked, "Why are there Iraqis in my tent?"

She shook her head and said, "There isn't enough room in the detainee tent and these guys need treatment."

Trying to hide my anger, I said, "Great."

She responded, "Don't worry, they're handcuffed to the bed, and there are MPs at each section."

I responded coolly, "It's not them attacking me that I am worried about."

She admonished, "Behave."

Deann was extremely attentive and was thrilled to be taking care of U.S. soldiers, which was a nice break from Iraqi detainees. She gave me great treatment—even though I incessantly requested sponge baths, which never happened. She changed my IV sites with the least pain I have ever had while having veins punctured. One of the first things she did was change my bandages to allow me to see my new stump. It looked as though it had been chopped off with an axe and beaten with a rubber hose. It was sewed up in a clean line that looked like the bottom of a bag of rice or oats. It looked surreal. But Deann explained it all. I spent most of the day and night sleeping, waking only long enough to give vitals and take pain medicine, morphine, and Percocet. It was a relief to sleep.

After my first long sleep, I sat up and thought about what the doctor had said, that I would be running in a year. I knew that overcoming this would be the biggest challenge in my life. I wasn't sure where to set my goals. I didn't know any amputees. I couldn't even imagine what a prosthesis looked or felt like. But running in a year, that seemed like a reasonable goal.

As I was contemplating all of this, my commander, Lieutenant Colonel Butch Kievenaar, came to visit me. As he and I share a sick sense of humor, he immediately came in joking.

With a smile, he said, "David, I know you want to get back to see that baby born, but this is going too far!"

He could not stay long, but he had come a long way to see me, and it meant the world to me.

The reason he came was to offer me some incentive. I had not yet been given my Officer Efficiency Report counseling, but the regimental commander wanted me to know that I needed to get healthy again so that I could take command of the regimental headquarters and headquarters troop. I was honored.

Even though I was filled with pride, the reality of the impossibility of the offer immediately kicked in. My own words, spoken just hours before, rang in my head: "I have given enough." Was the Army serious? Did my superiors not realize that I had just had my foot sawed off? It seemed ridiculous to think about. I was having a hard enough time in my heart bearing with the loss of my command; now they were offering me another. I thought, "Maybe they're just trying to keep me from killing myself, like these shrinks in here, telling me to think about all of the good things I should look forward to." But Lieutenant Colonel Kievenaar was a man of his word; he wasn't trying to feed me shit and call it sugar. It was something to think about and was certainly comforting to know that the regiment still wanted me on the team. I realized that someone was finally noticing all my hard work. But I had too much on my mind to give my future any more thought.

Lieutenant Colonel Kievenaar saw me wiping my tears, straining to come up with an answer, and told me, "Don't decide now. Go home and discuss it with Kim. Think about what is best for you. You have paid your dues to this Army, and nobody would think less of you if you decided to retire. I am proud of you, and was proud to serve with you in combat."

I asked my commander only for one thing, and that was my guidon, my unit flag. The outgoing commander, if he served honorably, usually received his colors as he left his unit. It was a tradition I wanted to live by. I had almost died for that flag, and wanted to take it home with me.

After he left, I lay there and thought about the idea of taking command again within the next year. It seemed so impossible. I had just pledged to run within the year, and now I was going to take command. I had to rethink my goals. Again, with nothing to go off of, it was quite difficult. So I thought about the year ahead. I thought surely within a few months I would be on prosthesis. So by Christmas, I would ski. By New Year's, I would snowboard. By February, I would pass an Army physical fitness test, be found fit for duty by the Army, then run two miles and take command by June. Lastly, I wanted to climb a 14,000-foot mountain by the end of September. I was so exhausted by setting goals that I went to sleep.

The next day, Jon Kluck arrived with my luggage and my guidon. I remember little about my visit with Jon. He did tell me how both my soldiers and the leaders in town were quite broken up about my injury. He told me that the mayor himself had found out who planted the mines and had given the information to my colonel. I suppose, as soon as he finished visiting me, Lieutenant Colonel Kievenaar had flown back and oversaw Killer conducting a raid on the men who planted the mine and planned the attack. Jon told me how well my men performed, how they raided and killed the attackers as they resisted. Although it meant an official end to my command, I could at least be redeployed proudly with my colors in hand, knowing that my attackers were worse off than I was.

■ ■ ■

By the afternoon of 23 June, only two days after the injury, I was off again in a chopper to Baghdad International Airport, where I slept for about three hours on the ground before I was loaded onto an Air Force jet en route to Qatar. I was given a dose of pain medicine before the flight, but by the time I got to Qatar, I was dying for more. In Qatar, we were loaded onto a hot ambulance bus, which hit every bump and finally ran out of gas. They decided to push us on gurneys the rest of the way, but not before they dropped me as they got me out of the ambulance. Once at the hospital, I was fed up.

But after some time and some medication, things all worked out, and I slept the entire night and next day until it was time to load. I was in a bed next to Sergeant Kinkaid of the British Special Forces. We exchanged some stories, but were both too drugged to get to know each other. We finally loaded on the airplane about 2230, but didn't take off until after about 0230. The airplane was so hot, and I remember sweating out some poison during those four hours. Fortunately, the nurses were forthcoming with the Percocet and morphine cocktails. I slept most of the way to Germany,

I arrived at Landstuhl the morning of 25 June and was rolled into a private room with a window that looked out onto a flower garden. Had it been a travel hostel, it would have been a nice visit. The temperature was only about seventy and had a nice breeze. It would blow the smell of flowers into my room. What a different place I was in then! I was in heaven. I nearly slept the first forty-eight hours there. Well, after the first twelve hours, I was back in surgery, but only had some minor work done, mainly just a clean-up. Fortunately, I lost the hard cast and had only a bandage wrap.

I started physical therapy right away. The nurse who worked with me (I don't recall her name) was the biggest Aggie freak I have ever met, but it was good to see a Texan. She was a reservist and an Aggie Corps instructor and physical therapy instructor at the A&M nursing school. She was great: She got me off my ass, stopped me from feeling sorry for myself, and made me exercise. It wasn't easy; I had been injured only a few days before and was still very weak. But she knew how important it was to get me on my feet—er, foot. She taught me how to use crutches, got me out of my room, and had me climbing stairs once a day for thirty minutes a session. She wrapped a thick belt around my waist and used it to support me. It was painful, and it was mentally and physically challenging. I was afraid to hurt myself. But she made me do it. She was truly a leader.

My favorite was a cute blonde nurse who gave me special attention. It's no wonder that Hemingway so often wrote about loving nurses. When you have returned from death's door, they are the angels who catch your fall. This young lady came in telling me about how strawberries were in bloom in Germany, and she had a large batch at home that was going to waste. I have never been subtle, so I told her that my favorite pie was strawberry. The next morning, she brought in a strawberry pie.

Another pleasant memory of Landstuhl was a visit from a dear friend, Bob Grimmer. Bob works for General Dynamics as an arms and ammunition dealer. He travels the world and flew through Germany to stop and see me. Bob and I were lieutenants at Fort Hood together. We have stories that can never be told. He has always been like a brother to me. Unfortunately, he is like a brother I don't get to see too often anymore. But in Bob's special way, he appeared in my room like a dream. Fortunately, I had slept for a few days and could actually visit with someone for more than ten minutes. The phone calls were becoming more and more difficult, and Bob's visit gave me the familiar human touch I was missing from home. As a former soldier, he knew to bring me books, magazines, and junk food.

Bob's visit gave me the first opportunity to talk to someone else about everything. As he left the service to pursue greener pastures (the green being money), he told me that I had that option too. I confided my concerns to him. He was honest with me and asked me where my heart was. For the first time in my adult life, I wasn't sure. I loved the Army, but I was full of uncertainty. I told him how it was hard to even think about the future, lying in a hospital bed so far away from a normal life. Although I had spent a lot of time thinking about my life, all that was really on my mind was Kim, home, and getting there. Seeing my frustration, he reminded me that with time the right decision would come to me.

I was only lucid for a few hours before I needed to doze off again, but it was an incredible visit. His departure was one I will never forget. Bob started to gather his things as I started to fight back sleep. I asked if he would move the chair he had been sitting in back into the corner. Obliging, he turned to pick up the chair. As he swung back around and lifted it to clear the bed, he swung the leg of the chair right into my bloody stump. After I screamed, I tried to console him, but he went running out the door. We laugh about that day now, and it is always worth a free beer or two.

Although it sounds like I was having a good time in Germany, I was ready to get home and see my wife. My treatment was complete. Trouble was, I was not healing there. I had to get to Walter Reed to get my final revising and shaping surgery in order to start healing. Every day in Germany was another away from Kim and my child, who was due any day. All they were waiting on was the queue for the flight. They had some trouble with the flights and things were pretty backed up. But after getting bumped three flights in a row, I decided that I needed to find out for myself what was holding me up.

I woke up on 1 July and felt strong. I crutched almost a mile down to the redeployment center to find out who was in charge of redeployment. Some lieutenant directed me to a specialist in charge of managing the manifest lists. I waited about ten minutes for him, and gave him my stare.

He finally acknowledged me. As I crutched up to his desk, I noticed a thick stack of paperwork with a note attached with big black letters on the front that said, "SPC—Who the fuck are these people? Where the fuck are they? Find them, and get them out of here!"

I pointed at the list and said slowly, "Rozelle, David M., Captain, U.S. Army. Get me to Walter Reed Medical Center."

He thumbed through the list, and as he reached the last page, he said, "Ah, here you are."

As I waited now for a confirmed flight, the reality of home set in: I was going to be back into my wife's arms again. She filled my thoughts.

I arrived at Walter Reed on 3 July 2003, and joined the rest of my amputee brethren on Ward 57. Upon arrival, I found out that I was under quarantine, and had cultures taken from my groin, armpits, and nose. The doctors were worried about some virus that lives in the Iraqi sand. Interesting. When people came into my room, they had to don a gown and gloves. I was just worried that my parents weren't going to feel comfortable embracing me after putting on so much protective gear. Again, I was embarrassed. But my nurse assured me that my parents didn't have to follow this rule as long as they weren't visiting other patients. Although Kim couldn't come due to her condition, my immediate family was able to come in her absence.

The good news was that, again, I had a nice room to myself. My first nurse, Sylvia, was my favorite. She was my nurse many nights, and was always on duty when I was recovering from surgery. Sylvia helped get me ready for my parents. She made sure that I was clean, and helped me take a shower and held me steady as I shaved with hot water. She then put me in bed, and said she would wake me as soon as they showed up, because she knew I needed to be rested. Another angel.

My parents brought Amy and arrived that afternoon. My mother was the first in the room.

After reminding me that she was going to get me through this, she was laughing and crying at the same time as she said, "I told you not to get off of your tank. You should have listened to your mother."

She was smiling, but crying, and repeated, "I told you not to get off of your tank."

Her hug felt so good. As we hugged, I saw my father's face, with a smile covering up concern.

He came over and hugged me and said, "Welcome home, son."

Although I had heard it a hundred times already, it never quite meant the same as it did from him. The three of us broke into tears, and my sister came walking in. I was sorry to already have a face covered with tears, but I think she was relieved, because she wanted to cry with me anyway.

She hugged me and said, "I'm so happy you are home. I've been so worried about you."

I shrugged and said, "Thanks for coming."

We talked away the rest of the day, at least the rest of it that I was awake. Every few hours I would drift off, and they knew it was time to give me a break. When I spoke, they listened intently and asked a million questions. Besides my letters, it was one of the first times they had talked to me since I deployed to Iraq. The few phone calls I managed to make were to Kim, and my parents were always getting secondhand reports. So they were pleased to have some time with me first. It was good to get a lot of stuff off my chest. I prayed with my dad over killing men, and he helped me talk about it. I told them about all my missions, my brave men, and the conditions. All most people want to know about Iraq is the heat. My dad brought some seafood in that night for dinner, and even smuggled in a beer for me. It was an honor to have my first beer with my father. We would have gotten away with it, too, but Dad spilled one of the cups of beer on the floor, and I had to have housekeeping come in and mop after they left. It was a relief having my family there, but I sure was missing Kim.

After I thought my parents had left, my dad came back in.

He said softly, "Dave, you still awake?"

I said, "Of course, a soldier never sleeps."

He came to the edge of my bed, put his hand on my head, looked in my eyes, and said, "David, you're a man now. I have never been as proud of you."

■　■　■

My doctors, Dr. (Major) Don Gajewski (aka Dr. G.) and Dr. Roxanne Wallace, were awesome. They were set on getting me home soon. Actually, everyone was so helpful about wanting to see me home. When the hospital commander came into my room to visit, he asked me if there was anything I needed. I told him that my wife was due any day, and I needed to go through an accelerated surgery program to get home. Between him and Dr. G., they got me home. But there were still three surgeries to conduct before I could leave. They were worried about me being strong enough—until they got to know me. As I was one of the first lower extremity amputees, and the first to get the Symes procedure (which saves the heel pad of your foot to cover the exposed bone after amputation), they were willing to experiment more with my progress.

With everyone's help, I felt like I was heading home soon. Then I fell. The morning of the Fourth of July, I fell trying to hop into the shower. I had asked my parents to take me around to see the national monuments from the car. My mother brought with her some freshly ironed civilian clothes from home. I wanted to shower and shave myself, and be dressed and ready when they came to pick me up. As I tried to move from the sink to the shower chair, I slipped and tried to catch myself with my stump.

It sounded like a side of beef falling and hitting the floor. It was just the sound of raw meat slapping against the tile.

I couldn't believe the pain. There was a bad spot on the stump that busted open. I lay there for a minute with blood spraying all over the wall and running down my leg. I was naked and ashamed on the bathroom floor, so instead of pulling the emergency cord, I crawled back to my bed and crawled under the sheets, applying pressure with some old bandages. The nurses responded to my emergency call and almost slipped on the foot-wide blood trail that I had left along the eight-foot stretch from the bathroom door to where I lay in my bed, like the blood trail of a wounded animal in the woods. The bleeding wouldn't stop, and the pain worsened. The doctors were called, and wrapped it back up and scheduled me for surgery the next day. The fall actually identified some bad tissue in my stump. So, in a way, it was advantageous, but it sure didn't feel like it.

My fall was a setback physically for only a few hours. But emotionally, it peeled back a layer of self-doubt and pity. I thought, "How can I even think about staying on active duty when I can't even take a shower by myself?" I started to notice how difficult everything was. Some of my most painful moments had been getting on and off the toilet. Certainly, I was in much better shape than most guys on the ward, but I felt so helpless. I felt as though the next guidon that had been held out to me was slowly slipping out of my hands.

After hours of thinking, my parents came to my rescue. We spent the afternoon driving around D.C., realizing that the Fourth of July could possibly be the worst time ever to drive in D.C. So we went to Georgetown and had lunch, then sat and listened to jazz at an outdoor bar and enjoyed some gelato. We then retreated to the air conditioning of the mall and I showed off my newly developed pictures from Iraq. Soon after, we headed to Chinatown and had some great eats. After the feast, we headed down to the Washington Monument, and stopped near the Capitol on Pennsylvania Avenue as traffic just stopped. Everyone abandoned their cars and walked out onto the lawn to watch the fireworks. I was originally going to go and sit with the Walter Reed veterans watching Dolly Parton, but didn't want to split up from the family. Although the view was partially obscured by the trees, it was incredible. I was finally celebrating freedom.

At the end, Amy hugged me and said, "That was for you."

Indeed it was.

■   ■   ■

I finally went into surgery on 6 July, and slept well beyond my medications. That night, I was in incredible pain and cried most of the night, unable to catch up on my medication cycle. Fortunately, Sylvia was on duty and did everything she could to make me comfortable. It helped me sleep but didn't help with the pain. The next day, I was back in surgery to cut higher on my stump in order to make my bones flat and sew my stitches through the bone. Yes, stitches through the bone—and another painful recovery. But it would help make me more comfortable in prosthesis. The next day, Amy stayed in my room all day and took care of me. It was nice to have my big sister taking care of me, and it was my final surgery.

After a few more days for the doctors to bless me as having had my final surgery, I was able to fly out the next morning. Walter Reed expedited my clearing the next morning, and got me off to the airport. It is especially noteworthy considering the guys I know at Walter Reed now don't get to make their first trip home for convalescent leave for at least a month. I was in and out in two weeks. I wasn't sure if I was ready myself, as I looked down and saw blood coming through my bandages, and my stump was twice its earlier size. But I was going to make it home for that baby, no matter what.

As I was racing home, I realized that I was passing up the world-class physical and occupational therapy treatment at Walter Reed, but I left with a promise. Both my doctor and the staff told me that I was forever welcome at Walter Reed for treatment. It was easier to leave knowing that my return was only a phone call away.

Once at the airport, I started to get a hero's treatment. Mom and I were able to get all my luggage through for no extra charge, and I sat first class. People applauded me as I passed through security. Everyone looked at me with pride. Nobody looked at me like a cripple, but as a war hero. I was proud, but tired.

I sat next to Senator John Kerry, the future Democratic presidential nominee, who introduced himself as a veteran. Our conversation was brief, but memorable, and ended with a bit of a pinprick in my pride.

I quote Kerry, who said, "I don't support the war, but I appreciate your sacrifice."

"Thanks." I didn't say another word the entire flight, but leaned back and slept, and that was my farewell to D.C.

It seemed that the next time I awoke, I was rolling down the jetway at Colorado Springs Airport. I could see Kim from far away. Kim looked beautiful and cried like a baby. Her mother told her once that she isn't pretty when she cries, so she tries not to, and I could see her fighting it off. Carolyn Kievenaar and Karen Chumbley were there as the cheering section, which was nice. Kim had flowers and a balloon for me. I really can't remember what was said at the airport or the way home. It is still like trying to remember a dream. I just wanted to get home, take some more painkillers, and get in my bed to sleep.

At the house, Kim and the girls had hung a banner across the garage: "Welcome Home Big Daddy!"

Finally, I was home.

CHAPTER 11

Recovery and Birth

JUST AS A NEW FIGHT HAD BEGUN for me in Iraq when the president had declared a major end to combat, I was now home and had another uncertain enemy to face. Although it was a relief to be in my own home with my own things, everything was a challenge. Something as simple as getting out of bed in the morning became a task; the idea of trying to get up usually kept me there for days at a time. My life was going to be different, and I wasn't willing to face facts.

My biggest problem was my addiction to morphine. I had been taking it for pain for more than a month. Fortunately, I was honest with myself and admitted that I wasn't going to be able to live without it. I needed it, and I wasn't hiding it. I was an addict, but thought more of it as a required addiction, to get me through. Morphine is a "saturating" drug. You have to take a lot for it to be effective, every one to three hours. If you let your level of morphine fall, you have to start the saturation cycle over. So in order for it to work continuously, you must maintain an addiction.

Even at night, I would roll over and wake up just long enough to take another dose. I was also taking Percocet, which added to my comfort. The problem, though, was that I was never comfortable. I could be lying perfectly relaxed, breathing and meditating, and still feel pain shooting up my legs, through my back, and into my head. Occasionally, phantom pains would stop me and bring tears to my eyes. In phantom pain, your nervous system still sends pain signals from a limb that doesn't exist; my nerves and brain had to adapt. Every day, five to ten times a day, I would have those phantom pains. They were intense, like the first pain I had felt in the back of the Humvee on the way to camp. The more drugs I took, the more comfortable I was.

But the phantom pains never went away. Even under heavy sedation, I could still feel pain in my toes. When I would wiggle them, the freshly attached muscle and tendon would pull taut and send shooting pains up my legs. More common were simple itches, which I could never scratch. Sometimes, I would even lie in bed and try to scratch my existing foot with what I thought was a foot and find nothing but a stump rubbing short. The pains would occasionally stop me in my tracks. I never quite learned to deal with them and maybe never will.

In an attempt to ease the pain during the first few days, I would have a beer, just because I could. I would have an ice-cold beer in a frozen mug. I would have it and think about my men in Iraq. Sort of cruel, I admit. But I was so doped, it seemed fun, but I couldn't feel the effects of the alcohol. After the first few beers, I decided drinking wasn't worth it. But after the first week home, I decided it was time to get drunk. My wife was out at a ladies' coffee, and I was home alone for the first time in four months. I drank the six beers in the fridge, and then raided the liquor cabinet. I should have been shitfaced, but was fine. Yes, I had done all that and continued to medicate myself. The only trouble I had was crutching around the house, as I was knocking stuff over and spilling my whiskey on the way back to the couch. The worst of it was the hangover I had the next day, which, of course, was cured with drugs.

By choice, I started a vicious and unforgiving cycle. I would get up late and stay up late. I was spending my days moving from the bed to the couch and watching movies all day and night. I had Kim wait on me, so nothing was too much effort on me. I watched nothing but war movies. I was worthless. The only chore I did was to go out to the mailbox to get the mail, in order to see which friend had written to me. Each day I returned with my pockets stuffed with cards and collected them like every day was my birthday. I wouldn't even talk to my own wife, but lived to see what letters came each day. I was tired, felt I deserved a break, and wanted people to take care of me.

I got stacks of letters and packages from friends and family. I got letters from Army buddies, Air Force buddies, old teachers, ministers, girlfriends, classmates, and sports teammates. Each praised my undying spirit, and each knew I would overcome my injury. Many people wrote that if it were to happen to anyone, I was the best suited to overcome it. I received so much praise. One friend wouldn't even tell me that he had earned a Purple Heart, because he felt he didn't deserve it compared to me. I was flattered, and realized how loved I was by so many. It reminded me that I had friends all over the world. I got e-mails and calls from Germany, France, Great Britain, Korea, China, Australia, New Zealand, and Mexico.

Fortunately, all these friends and admirers couldn't see me crying on the couch, feeling sorry for myself. I realized how worthless I was becoming, but I felt like I deserved it. I wasn't telling Kim my stories from the war and wasn't sharing my feelings about combat or my injury with her. I hadn't even found the words yet to tell her how I had killed other men. She would often find me lying there crying, ask me what was wrong, and I would push her away. The only way she heard about my actions in Iraq was during phone interviews or overhearing me as I talked to friends. At a time where we should have been closer than ever, we were drifting apart.

Then, after the second week, *my* letter came—the last one I wrote to Kim before my injury. Most newspapers around the country have printed the last letters of soldiers who died in combat. I even started collecting the articles that had them reprinted. It was fascinating to me to see what people wrote home about and what their last words were to their family. In my drugged state, I had forgotten to expect my own. Had I died, my letter would have been the last words that Kim ever read from my hand. The day it came was the same as any other. I woke and got out of bed about 1000 hours and promptly moved to the couch to have some coffee and prepare for another day in front of the television. At mail time, I crutched out and gathered the letters. Back at the house, I got a beer and went into the living room to see what I got. And there it was, written on 19 June 2003, what could have been my last words.

Dream Girl,

Well, I waited and waited, and it was well worth the wait. Thank you for my care package. Yours is the best care package ever. Thank you for everything, you are the greatest.

I immediately tore into the dried fruit. That is a good brand, and I see you found the natural foods market. Yummy, thanks. I can't wait to try the coffee. I will probably try it in the morning. I have been running in the mornings, so my body is usually too hot for brewed coffee. On my days off from training I brew some up. I am afraid I will have to share most of it, because lots of people have been eyeballing it. That is fine though, because everyone seems to be sharing everything they get too.

I love the anniversary card. I love the tradition we have [of inserting a picture that represents the year in one of our wedding invitations]. I am also glad you chose that picture for our Christmas card. I don't think most people know what a huge accomplishment it is to climb a '14-er.' I am glad that you share that hobby with me, and I with you. I think hiking will be one we do forever, especially with the kids. Sundays will most certainly include a family hike.

What I love most are the traditions that you have started with me. The anniversary and Christmas cards are just my favorite examples. I hope that I am home soon enough for this year's card.

If not, I think you should send a good one of the baby. But if I am home, I think we should return to our theme and have three sets of feet hanging out in front of some incredible Colorado scenery. If the baby is alone in the picture, I think you should get a shot of it rolling around in the aspen leaves. With your new digital camera, you can shoot again and again until you get the perfect shot. I hope I am home to help, even if it is a New Year's card, or later. I can just imagine our feet, and two little feet sticking up out of nowhere. That will be so cute. Then again, getting those little feet to cooperate may be more difficult than it sounds. We'll see.

I love the 3D ultrasound photographs. I guess there is a story behind them. How did you work that? I wish I had been there to sing, "The first time . . . ever I saw your face." I bet you cried, because I did here. Some of them are like those magic eye posters, and are difficult to see. But some are really incredible, and I can see Boo smiling at me. I can clearly see the nose, which could easily resemble either of us, and only hope it is not too big. For some reason, the pictures make me think it is a boy. I am not sure why, but I just had this feeling. It is funny how indifferent I am about which it is. I originally hoped that it was a girl, but am equally excited now that I think it is a boy. God, I can't wait. You must notify me immediately. I am not sure how immediate that will be, but I will call you as soon as I know. I wish I could see you now, eight months pregnant. I bet you are cute as a button. I hope you are getting some good pictures. Don't be embarrassed about any of it; rather be proud of your motherhood. I am sure both you and the baby will be healthy. I wonder if you are going to be breastfeeding when I get home. Anyway, thanks for the 3D images, what a treat.

Your pre–Father's Day card was quite thoughtful. I know that you are proud to carry my child. Although it is difficult, I know that you are proud to say that the father is off at war. It is amazing how our love can get stronger. I guess that having a child together will do that to you. I was just the other day dreaming about what an awesome mix our child will be: your compassion and my emotion, your study habits and my intelligence, your science and my art, your strength and my balance, your smile and my eyes. It is going to be incredible to watch us in a baby grow. I have such dreams for Boo, and can't wait to share them all with you.

Oh, and when I asked for a baby book, I did not mean a book on changing diapers, but for a book on psychology. I am not sure what a good author is for children, or who matches our ideology, but we can only find out by reading. Anyway, that's what I meant. Although I think I am ready, coming home to a baby is like deploying to this war. I am just going to have to jump in and figure it out as I go along. I would rather dodge poo than bullets anytime.

Thank you so much for the goodies. I will write on the labels of the cigars what I think of each. I am waiting until next month to smoke them, but I already added water to the humidor sponge. They still feel fresh and smell delicious. I can't wait to smoke them. I plan on sharing a few, but not all of them. I am going to be selfish on those devils.

Take care of yourself and Boo. Give Rider my love. I am doing fine and actually enjoyed hearing you break down on the phone the other day. I needed to hear that as badly as you needed to let it out. I know you were upset about losing your composure, but it was important to me. I love you so much, and know you worry about me. My men are taking great care of me, and I to them. Send my love to the family.

All my love,

David

As I finished, Kim came downstairs and asked me what we got. I was broken. As I looked into her caring eyes, I knew it was time to get back to life. I owed it to her, the child, and myself.

■ ■ ■

As I started to think about family, I realized how selfish I had been. I considered one option, staying on active duty, and what that could mean for my career and me. But it wasn't just about me. It was supposed to be a family decision. The only time Kim and I talked about it was when I told her, "I have given enough." Because I hadn't opened up to her, she really had no idea about all the time I spent thinking about the future. It was time to talk, and we finally did. In the end, all she wanted for me was to choose what I felt in my heart was best for me. Again, I had to confess to her and to myself that I didn't know.

At this point, people were starting to throw some pretty interesting job offers my way. As they came, I started keeping a journal about the pros and cons of staying in the military versus becoming a civilian. I couldn't imagine being a civilian, but I at least wanted to give it a fair review. That's really all I gave it, as I couldn't think of any other profession that would give me the satisfaction of being in the Army. I enjoyed being a leader of men. Cavalrymen.

But there was still a decision I had no control over, and that was the Army's decision about me. The truth is, I could not seriously consider another career until that question was resolved. Despite my obligation to consider my family, I was still being selfish. I kept asking myself, "What is going to make *me* happy?"

■ ■ ■

Physical therapy was a total lifesaver for me. I had done it from the beginning. Outside of Baghdad, I had lain in my bed doing abdominal stretches and shoulder and neck rotations, which helped reduce the stress. It was actually a relief for me in Landsthul to be able to do push-ups and sit-ups in bed. I really wanted to do pull-ups, but I was too weak. I spent most of my time on crutches, but my crushed left toe kept me from overdoing it. At Walter Reed, I quickly learned the physical therapy routines and was working by myself from the start. I was thrilled to have the strength to lift weights for my upper body. Stretching was relaxing and therapeutic as well. After the final surgery, I got my take-home instructions for physical therapy. It was my goal to be out of a wheelchair before I left Walter Reed, and I was ready for it. But at home I was getting lazy.

I knew that I would enjoy the physical therapy at home. It replaced the gap in my normal schedule of conducting physical training every morning. But before I could start getting myself into shape,

I had to beat my drug habit. I was so sluggish and easily fatigued. I knew it was the drugs dragging me down, but I was afraid of the pain. I went to my doctor and told him I wanted to quit the pain medication. He completely agreed and was relieved at my decision. Although he thought it was a bit soon, especially since the stitches were still fresh, he recommended a subtle regimen of lowering my doses, until I was taking only Tylenol and Motrin.

I decided to go cold turkey and almost killed myself in the process. I was sick for a week. I had incredible abdominal pain and was blowing out both ends. To add to it, the pain in my stump was unbearable, and I was getting phantom pains every five minutes. I was really sick, but after a week I was clean. Most important, I was happy.

Once off the drugs, I was able to medicate a little more with my old friend the bottle. Kim kept an eye on me; it seemed that I was replacing one addiction with another over a week's time. It wasn't until she said something to me that I realized that although I was happy and active, I was also drunk most of the time. So I cut back. It was a battle that was much easier to win and had fewer physical side effects.

Exercise was my savior, as it replaced my addiction. Kim was due any day, and we had to make many trips to the hospital for the both of us. I would do two hours of stretching and physical therapy at home, then lift weights in the basement of the hospital. After that I would meet Kim for her appointments, or attend mine before lunch. The first week completely exhausted and frustrated me, but helped me sleep at night. I refused to quit, so I was hopping all over the gym. My cardio routine was just getting from one machine to the other. I wanted to lift free weights, but didn't have the strength to hop around with the larger weights, and couldn't afford to fall. I was weak, but made progress every time I entered the gym.

After all the time in the hospital and after beating the morphine I only weighed 175 pounds. When I had deployed to Iraq, I had been about 220. People didn't even recognize me when I got home. I was sickly skinny. But I was drug-free and ready to get my body where it needed to be to accomplish my goals.

My doctor told me, "If you want to ski again, you have to be in the best shape of your life."

More important was Kim's challenge: "I want your chest and arms back."

I took both comments to heart and got started.

■ ■ ■

After weeks of waiting, and the due date one week past, Kim finally announced that the baby was ready to arrive. Kim's mother, Donna, was in town for the birth. She had already been there for two weeks and had to extend her ticket to hang around for the actual birth. Thank goodness she did. Those two weeks gave Kim a break from taking care of me, and gave her a hand preparing the house for a new baby. Even though I was on track to improvement, I had no foot, which made my leg worthless, and still spent most of the day on the couch. Toward the end of her first week, I had Donna convinced that it was okay for me to drink my first cocktail at lunch.

With a deadline for Donna's departure on 8 August, we combed the books for old remedies to produce labor. Kim and I tried everything: long walks, bumpy roads, herbal teas, cold showers, and sex—you name it. Some of it was fun, but none of it worked.

The worst was going to Hooters. Spicy food is supposed to encourage labor in pregnant women. So there I was, with my pregnant wife and mother-in-law, at Hooters. Upon arrival, Kim announced to our waitress that she needed the spiciest wings on the menu in hopes of going into labor. So rather than bending over my table and flirting with me while she took our order, I got ten minutes of history on all the girls in the place who were pregnant or just had kids. I had gone to Hooters for the last three years for lunch with my mechanics, and it was one of those places where a married man can enjoy the view without getting in trouble. It took ten minutes to ruin that romance. Oh, and no labor, just heartburn.

On 4 August, Kim woke up and was determined to have that baby. Her doctors had promised us that if she wasn't ready then, they would induce, based on her low embryonic fluid levels. We were a sight. Kim had packed everything in the car and was ready to move in. Once at the hospital, they told us that she was so close to going naturally that they were not going to induce. I said nothing, but loaded all the stuff back in the car. We went home and ate leftover chicken wings.

By mid-afternoon Kim was in full labor, and we packed it up again for the hospital. This time, she was effaced and dilated, so she was admitted. I set up the room and went to get food. By the time I got back, they were ready for the epidural. Kim had never had any kind of pain like that before, so when they asked her what her pain level was on a one-to-ten scale, she said eight. So they dosed her epidural to what she thought was an eight. Unfortunately, her pain was just beginning.

When the doctors came to check on Kim, they saw her leaning back, breathing hard, and me with my swollen and throbbing foot propped up on the stirrup, and wouldn't know who to attend to. We were quite a sight.

I tried to get some sleep, and napped on a rollout bed from ten until about midnight.

At midnight, the nurse woke me up and said, "It's time, and we need your help."

And so I witnessed the miracle of birth. It was easier to see dead people than it was watching birth. For two hours I stared at Kim, saying, "Oh ... I see it ... keep going ... it's almost there." But it wasn't, and Kim hated me. She told me later that she wished that I had been in Iraq, because I would have been more help there than in the delivery room.

At 0214 hours on 5 August 2004, Forrest Sumpter Rozelle slipped headfirst into our lives.

As soon as I saw him, I yelled, "It's a boy."

We had read in the books that healthy babies come out crying. Forrest was silent and still. He was purple and not breathing well on his own, as he had inhaled his own feces inside the womb. They took him to a warming table and sucked out his mouth and nasal passages and got him going. I came forward to cut his umbilical cord, and then escorted him to baby intensive care for his first shots, bath, and record creation. I gave him his first bath, and he hated it. At this point, I had forgotten all about Kim. It was all about the baby boy.

After about an hour of shots and warming, Forrest looked like a healthy baby, so we returned to find Kim for his first meal. She was

sleeping, but was happy to see him again. My parents were also there, waiting to see their first grandchild. He had his first meal and both mother and
child fell asleep. Kim had some bleeding and had to stay in ICU for observation, so I tried to sneak into our room and get some sleep.

I actually spent about an hour on the phone calling all the family about the birthday of the baby boy before the door opened and the
nurse pushed in a rolling newborn crib with Forrest. I looked behind
her and didn't see Kim rolling in.

"Hello, Daddy," said the nurse.

Concerned, I asked the nurse, "Where is Kim?"

She responded, "Mom is getting some well-deserved rest, so you
are in charge of the baby."

My heart stopped, and I said, "By myself?"

She laughed and said, "Yes!"

Even more worried, I said, "I don't know what to do."

She said, "You have to learn sometime. You might as well learn
today."

I looked down at Forrest and then looked back to her, just as she
walked out the door. I stayed awake and stared at Forrest for three
hours. About every ten minutes, I would put my hand on him to make
sure he was alive, then lie back down and watch him sleep. He was perfect, and he was my son.

■ ■ ■

After the normal two days of recovery in the hospital, we brought Forrest home. It was the second homecoming from a hospital I had expe-

rienced in a month. This time was even more emotional as we carried Forrest up to his room and put him to bed. We were home for the first time as a family. After helping us settle for the first few days at home, Kim's mother had gone home, and my parents pleaded with us to go to dinner together while they drove around the block, keeping Forrest asleep with the movement of the car.

When we first sat down at the steakhouse, I thought things were going to go badly. Kim was crying and I was in pain. Just as most new mothers do, Kim missed the baby and was struck with panic being away from him for the first time. I took out a picture of Forrest and leaned it up against a saltshaker in front of Kim. Our waitress probably thought we were trying to get a free meal. After I explained that it was our first night out since the birth of our baby, Kim told her that it was also our belated anniversary dinner, since I had spent our anniversary in Germany after getting blown up by a mine. We didn't get a free meal, but we got a free dessert. More important, we actually looked into each other's eyes and talked for the first time since I had come home. That dinner was one of the most important meals of our relationship. It was only the first step toward the kind of counseling we needed, but was at least the beginning of our communication.

Just as we were getting used to being home together as a family and creating a schedule for Forrest, I got a call from the White House. The Army had chosen me to be a greeter for the president during his visit to Denver in a few days, and the White House wanted to assure me that my family was also welcome to attend. I had only been home for three weeks, but we were thrilled. It put us in a whirlwind of preparation. I hadn't worn a uniform since the last one was cut off me in

Iraq, Kim had just had a baby and had no dress clothes that would fit, and the baby was going to be less than a week old. None of that stopped us. Mom took Kim shopping and got her a new outfit. I dusted off my dress uniform and tried to make it look presentable for a presidential review. The baby was the easiest to prepare, as all we had to do was buy some sunscreen and pick out his best outfit.

After passing through some rather thorough security, we were able to move to the waiting area with the rest of the dignitaries. Yes, even the baby was screened. (He passed.) We waited for an hour before Air Force One landed and we then marched out onto the tarmac. We lined up and I was positioned last in line so that I could have the most time with the president. The door opened and he stepped out, waving like a president should wave to the people: standing strong and proud.

Kim whispered into my ear, "Aren't you nervous?"

Well, I hadn't been, but I was for a brief second after she asked. Then I looked down at Forrest sleeping on her chest, just six days old, without a care in the world.

I looked back up at Kim and said, "I wasn't … but I'm fine. He's just another man."

The president made his way down the line, and I tried to maintain my military bearing, as it was tempting to watch him greet and talk to everyone in line. With him were Senator Ben Nighthorse Campbell of Colorado and Condoleezza Rice, one of my favorites on his staff.

As he got closer, my military bearing improved and I came to attention, as well as I could on one leg with crutches.

When he turned to me, I saluted and said, "Brave Rifles, Sir!"

He returned my salute, just as any soldier would, and I thought, "He is the commander in chief, not someone trying to be it."

He said, "How are you, Captain?"

I responded, "Fine, Mr. President."

He stopped, put his hand on my shoulder, looked into my eyes, and said, "No, really, Rozelle ... how are you doing?"

I was dumbfounded for a minute, because I had the president in front of me, not exchanging chitchat, but asking me how I was doing.

"Really, fine, sir. I survived the war, I am going to be back on my feet in no time, and my wife just had a baby boy."

"Well, Captain, you have the spirit. Are you a runner?"

"Yes, sir, I am."

"Well, when you get well enough, I want to have you down to Crawford for a run."

"I would be honored, Mr. President."

He looked into my eyes again, grabbed my hand, and said, "I am proud of you, son."

I turned to my wife and said, "I am honored to introduce you to my wife, Kimberly, and my six-day-old son, Forrest."

He put his hand on Forrest's back and replied, "Six days old, wow ... congratulations."

Kim replied, "Yes, born August 5."

Then he looked into Kim's eyes and asked, "How are you handling all this?"

Kim said, "We are really doing fine."

The president added, "The country is grateful for your sacrifices, and owes you a debt of gratitude. Thank you for being there for him. Your country thanks you."

Kim was visibly shocked at such kind words, and replied, "Thank you."

Then, the president turned back to Condoleezza Rice and said, "Condi, you need to come meet this captain."

As she approached, I shook Senator Campbell's hand, and he said, "We are proud of you. Are you from Colorado Springs?"

I responded, "Yes, Senator, from Fort Carson."

Then Condoleezza Rice approached and said, "Thank you for your sacrifice."

I responded, "It was my honor."

"We are very proud of you and your willingness to serve," she added.

I introduced her to Kimberly and Forrest.

Ms. Rice asked, "How old?"

Kim said, "Six days old. I wouldn't have missed this."

Ms. Rice said, "Thank you for your service. We appreciate what you do."

As soon as Condoleezza Rice had a good look at the baby, the president was back and said, "Rozelle, I am counting on you to get yourself in shape for this run. You'll be with the 100 degree club, just don't start running faster than an eight-minute mile."

I said, "Yes, sir, I'm counting on it."

He said, "Take care of your wife and baby."

As he climbed into his limousine, I saluted and said, "Yes, sir. Veterans!"

As soon as he drove away, the Secret Service agents asked me if we would like to tour Air Force One. I am not sure if anyone has ever turned down that opportunity, and neither did we. Air Force One is incredibly nice and plush. Anything the president touches must have the presidential seal on it. The seal was everywhere. Due to security reasons, we were not able to take photographs on board the aircraft. When we toured the president's chambers, they let us set Forrest in the president's chair. I even called my dad on his cell phone from the president's personal line, because I knew Dad would get a kick out of that.

But as we walked through the plane, I was in a bit of a daze. All I could think about was running with the president. I had set so many goals for myself, and now I had another important goal. I had to get in shape, but I had to first get a leg.

■　■　■

Two days after meeting the president, I met Chris Jones, a certified orthotist and prosthetist. From the time of my injury, I had tried to imagine what a prosthesis would feel like. I had heard from doctors that your body adjusts to it, and before you know it, you don't even know it's there. I was afraid that those were the words of people with two legs trying to imagine what it's like to wear a prosthetic limb. I can tell you now that you are always aware of your prosthesis. Even when it is the most comfortable, it never feels like your real foot. And at times it can be unbearable.

Chris was extremely excited about helping me. He spent lots of time showing me different feet and telling me about ideas he had. His enthusiasm was obvious and refreshing. Prosthetists don't usually get to work with young people who are able to really test their technical abilities and creative development. For example, most Symes amputees are older diabetics who have lost circulation in their feet. They generally want something that is going to get them around to run errands, and that's about as active as they need to be. As soon as I walked in the door, I told Chris that I wanted to run, be fit for duty, and play rugby, all within the year. I am a prosthetist's dream because I will push anything they give me to its limits and beyond.

Chris and I have become good friends. My doctor at Walter Reed told me to find a prosthetist that I like, befriend him, and stay with him. A prosthetist must know how you walk, jump, run, dance, ski, and fall. On a number of occasions, we have had to go and "field test" my leg in a number of different environments: like skiing, snowboarding, pub-crawling, and parties. He knows me maybe too well.

The day I was to walk for the first time on my injured leg was months earlier than I had originally been told. Kim, Forrest, and I went to Chris's shop in Colorado Springs during the last week of August and met my new foot.

I found it uncomfortable and difficult to walk on. It was not the perfect replacement I'd been dreaming about for two and a half months. Yes, I was going to have to learn to walk on it. But even that first day, I was soon strolling up and down the hall without any support. It was like any other sport; it just took a few passes to figure out the muscle motion, and I was off to the races. After only about a half hour of adjustments, I was outside jumping, walking steps, doing push-ups, and sprinting up small inclines. We were still identifying all the hot spots, but I was fully functional.

I had a new son, I was off the painkillers, I had my stitches out, I had a new foot, there were only three months before ski season, the president had challenged me to a run by spring, and I had fewer than ten months to get in shape to take another command. I had lots of work to do.

■   ■   ■

The week I met my new foot, Lee Cowan, a reporter for CBS, followed me around for a week at Fort Carson. Because of some newspaper stories about my injury, America was interested in my recovery. I was honored and was surprised that I felt remarkably comfortable in front of the camera. I was proud and felt that I was sending a positive message to the American people. The Army hadn't always had good press, as the media felt it necessary to invade the lives of families of fallen soldiers and put them on display—not as a tribute, but as a way to taint public opinion against the war. I was sick of the politically driven negative propaganda and was tired of seeing the faces and stories of dead soldiers exploited. It angered me and it was not in the historic spirit of honoring dead soldiers. So I felt that I could tell a story of success.

The headline on several stories was (and I paraphrase), "Injured Soldier Wants to Return to Iraq." That bothered me. I was a proud veteran and supported my fellow troops in Iraq, but I was certainly not dying to go back. My message was getting misinterpreted. Truly, if I was found fit for duty, I knew that the odds of returning were favorable. But I had just received my new foot and couldn't even imagine going back to Iraq. More important, I wasn't even sure if the Army was going to let me go at all. The story was really about me getting my foot and my long road to recovery. My decision to stay in the Army and to go back to Iraq was still months away.

No soldier wants to go to war. War is a last option. But soldiers always maintain their war-fighting skills, and when called, they are ready to serve. I did long to rejoin my soldiers. I had promised the families of Killer that I would bring them home, and I felt I had let them down. But right now my place was at home, to heal. Once in shape to fight again I would be ready to fight and give my life. But first things first.

CHAPTER 12

My New Mission: Amputee Support

S OON I REALIZED THAT I WAS VIEWED as an "American hero." I did not consider myself one, but it was in my face. Everywhere I went, people were stopping to thank me for my service. Some would cry at seeing me, and some older veterans would stop and salute me. I couldn't go anywhere near a bar without getting a free drink. It wasn't like I was wearing a T-shirt with "Disabled Vet" on the front, but I live in a military town and people read between the lines. I was honored.

Kids had the funniest reaction to me. Most would stop whatever they were doing and stare. Not just a glance, but an "I can't blink my eyes because I'm looking so hard" stare. My friend Laura, who studies child psychology, said that limb loss is the single most terrifying thing for children to comprehend. It must be, because I could stop kids at a full run.

Sometimes I felt like the Pied Piper of kids. They would follow me down the street or through the mall. They could also be pretty mean.

It was common to hear them say, "Hey, look at that freak with no foot. . . . Wow!"

I usually shrugged it off, and dismissed it as kids being kids. But there were a couple of instances where the comments really hurt my feelings.

I was on my way to my mailbox and heard, "Look, it's that one-legged freak."

They all gathered around and were chasing me to the mailbox, cutting me off to ask questions and bending over to get a good look at it. They encircled me and were laughing and pointing. I must admit that whacking them with my crutches was next on my list, but Kim came running out and chased them away.

She screamed, "It's not nice to talk and stare at other people! That is very mean. I don't ever want to see you do that again. Now you go home before I call your mothers."

That was pitiful, but I gave it back a little, I must admit. There was one time some children were following me down the street, and I stopped to let them look.

One asked, "Hey mister, where's your foot?"

To Kim's dismay, I said, "Oh my goodness, it must have fallen off again! Can you guys help me find it?"

Those kids spread out and searched the whole street and part of the park before their parents stopped them.

The worst is the ignorance of adults. People feel free to ask me what happened, and then give me their whole philosophy on war, both for or against. What people don't understand is that there was nothing political about my getting blown up—it was an act of terrorism.

Most conversations go like this:

"Excuse me, but what happened to you?"

I respond, "I lost my foot to an injury in the war."

Most respond to me with, "What war?"

Those who need explanation of what war are usually satisfied with it, and often say, "Welcome home, soldier," "Thank you, soldier," or "God bless you."

My favorite response was, "Wow, thanks. Bartender, give this guy whatever he wants, on me!"

Every now and again, I would get the standard, "That is horrible. How do you feel about the war?"

I would give them my stone-faced look and say, "How do you feel about your freedom? If you aren't willing to die for it, then you aren't American."

My cousin Stewart's favorite was the time we were fishing in South Carolina and someone came over and asked, "What happened to you, son? That's a hell of a limp!"

Trying to focus on fishing, I responded only, "Iraq."

To which he said, "Damn, a wreck, you a race car driver or something?"

I laughed and said, "Yeah, something like that."

But all in all, I would say that America has made a 180 in its response to returning veterans, in just a single generation. And so have the soldiers. My father told me stories from the Vietnam era about people egging his car as he left base and spitting on soldiers when they went to town in uniform. But these days, I haven't seen that. Also, there are no stories about officers throwing away their medals on national television. Our soldiers are proud to defend their country against terrorism, and would not disrespect those still fighting by doing something so dishonorable. Soldiers are walking around with chests stuck out, showing off their medals. Colorado Springs even put on its first ticker-tape parade for our soldiers since World War II. The community has thrown us big parties, restaurants have offered free meals, businesses have given us great specials, and cops have even let us off tickets.

The best deal was when soldiers were able to make it home in time for the last few weeks of the 2003–2004 ski season, and Vail Resorts responded. As most soldiers were gone for the year, none had their regular season passes, and most felt like they had missed the season. Let me tell you, there are a lot of soldiers who chose Fort Carson for its proximity to the mountains, and especially for the skiing. To miss an entire ski season is a real bummer. Vail Resorts offered our soldiers up to four free nights of lodging and skiing at any of the Vail Resort lodges and mountains. The deal almost sounded too good to believe, and it was extended to all redeploying soldiers. I knew soldiers from field grade officers down to the lowest private who took advantage of the offer. Those few days made up for a year without snow. Colorado was a great place to be a soldier returning from war.

■   ■   ■

Although I was enjoying the honor our country had bestowed on me as a returning veteran, I was stunned with shock the day I realized that

I was an amputee. I know that sounds funny, but I didn't realize it the night I awoke from my first surgery. It wasn't the day I fell at Walter Reed and watched the blood soak my bed as I reached for the panic button. Rather, it was a day in September, sitting on the couch, sipping a cup of coffee, and resting my leg after a morning workout on my prosthesis.

From the time of my injury, I waited and waited for this magic prosthesis that was going to make me feel healed. I was ready to be healed. The doctors had already pulled the stitches out of the bone, and the skin flap took to the bone. I knew it was strong because I had fallen on my stump several times without tearing the flap open. Once I had the prosthesis and learned how it worked, I realized immediately that my injury wasn't a quick fix. The prosthesis wasn't just a cast that I would learn to walk on and then have it sawed off when I was better. It was permanent. It was frustrating. It was hard.

To start, you have to bear weight on sections of your leg that normally act to propel the foot. Now that tissue is merely weight-supporting, to relieve any pressure from the stump. All your force and drive comes from your thighs. Learning to walk on it was difficult enough. But I was also working out almost four hours a day. I wasn't gently breaking my new foot in. That day, I had done an especially hard workout on the stairmaster, jumped on the stationary bike for an hour, and then rode my mountain bike home from the gym. I was lying on the couch, icing my leg, and it hit me.

"I'm going to be like this forever."

It was like getting struck by lightning. It finally sank in all at once. It was good that I was alone, because I really got to cry it out. My brain was no longer hazy with the deception of drugs. It was clear to me that I was going to have to wear that fucking prosthesis all the time. Chris wasn't lying when he had said that I wouldn't be 100 percent for a year. It was going to take a year just to get used to living as an amputee. Whenever I went swimming, I would have to plan a safe place to take the prosthesis off, have a safe place to store it, and have the right things at hand to put it back on correctly. When I went fishing, I would have to take a water leg or stay on shore. I was slowly realizing that I was going to have to adapt my lifestyle. My heart broke.

Then I thought to myself, how am I going to do it? How am I going to get back to active duty? I would have to apply for a ruling by the Army's Medical Evaluation Board to be declared fit for duty to continue my Army career. But it seemed impossible at that moment. I was worried about my future and my family. I felt I had written a check that my body couldn't cash.

It was after that day that my mind started to heal. Before my day of self-realization, I dreamed about myself as able. In my dreams, I had two healthy legs and was free to do everything I missed. Even in my nightmares, I had full function of both legs. But then, after my epiphany, I dreamed about having one foot. I started dreaming about hopping around the soccer field, striking the ball into the goal and falling to the ground. I dreamed one night about charging (hopping toward) an enemy position with bayonet fixed and killing three Iraqi soldiers. I woke that morning proud of the fact that I was overcoming my personal demons. I was starting to accept myself. I was starting to deal with my new life.

As I got used to the prosthesis, I started dreaming about life with it. I dreamed about skiing and running. I stopped dreaming about combat and frustration, and started dreaming about my future. It was an emotional relief to have my dreams change, and it played out in my life.

About the same time as my dreams changed, so did my attitude. I was forced to act like my old self again in a social setting. I went on my first trip by myself to see my friend Josh play in a rugby tournament in Breckenridge, Colorado. It was my first time in the mountains, and as I crossed Indiana Pass, I screamed out loud. As upset as I had been just days earlier about the realization of my foot loss, I was now crying and shouting out for joy. I was alive. The mountains had never been so beautiful. As I crested the pass, I was above the tree line and could see the surrounding mountains and passes. There was hardly a cloud in the sky, and I could see every turned stone and bent tree. Wiping away the tears, I sang along with the band Phish, "I'm free!"

It was a proud moment for me to walk out onto the rugby field with my new leg, but what Josh made me do that night took me to a new level of healing. Ruggers are notorious for their parties. We basically took over Breckenridge. Lock up the women and children if there's a rugby tournament in town. I won't bore you with the details of my consumption, but I will tell you that I represented the Armed Services well in several "boat races." After we drained the kegs, some of the guys wanted to bar hop. I had already overworn my leg and was now on crutches. By the time we reached the dance club at the top of the hill, I was exhausted. While the rest were out jumping around with the girls on the dance floor, I sat nursing a Budweiser, watching things shake up.

Josh came over and said, "David, it's not like you to just sit there. Get your butt out here."

Frustrated, I looked at him and pointed at my crutches, saying, "Nobody wants to dance with a guy out there on crutches."

He gave me a strange look, then pointed over at a group of three good-looking girls dancing by themselves and said, "They do!"

I defended myself with, "I can't even dance on crutches!"

He pulled me up from the bar stool, placed the crutches under my shoulders, and said, "You're going to have to learn sometime. So get out there and learn."

I did get out there and hop around with those girls. It was harmless and fun, and I felt like the old Dave again. Most important, I got up, and realized what a true friend Josh Bodden was, and always will be.

■ ■ ■

It was now late September, and after returning from the mountains, I took time to make some realizations. I had left Walter Reed unarmed with what I needed to heal. There was no established support system to take care of me. I was doing a lot of self-discovery and was strong enough to overcome even the most severe trauma largely by myself. But I still had so many questions. I wondered how many of us had made it through the system and were now at home, recovering, but having trouble with their own realizations. I was lucky I had a friend like Josh who told me to get up. Not everyone has those friends, but in the Army we have each other.

Around this time I met a Symes amputee. He was a traveling salesman for a prosthetic foot company. I never would have guessed him to be an amputee. When we were introduced, he told me that he had the same amputation as I did, from birth.

It was a moment I had been looking for during the last three months, but all I could think to ask was, "What can't you do?"

He said, "There's nothing I can't do."

My moment to ask the hundreds of questions was lost. He was on a sales call and wasn't there to provide me counseling. He left just as quickly as he had come. The entire ride home, I thought again of all the questions I wanted to ask. Once home, I thought of all the unknowns that I had had from the beginning and wrote them down: How long does it take for the flap to fully heal? When can you crutch all day without spending the rest of the night suffering from a swollen stump? These were the answers I was dying to know. I decided to answer them myself. Over the next few weeks, I wrote down all the questions I had about the next year, leaving blanks for my answers. Slowly, I began to fill them in as they came to me, either through personal experience or outside sources. It has been a critical portion of my journal.

It was the e-mail from Vail Resorts about Colorado ski passes that really sent me rolling. It dawned on me that I had only two months before the ski season began. I was getting in shape, but my first goal was coming due. I couldn't even wear my leg all day, but I was supposed to ski? I immediately researched the Vail Adaptive Program and called the director, Ruth DeMuth. She was quite helpful and has since become a dear friend. She told me that it would be unwise for me to ski by myself and recommended I attend the Disabled Sports USA (DSUSA) clinic. I purchased my disabled pass and started to research DSUSA.

Logging onto their website (www.dsusa.org) was an eye-opening experience. I saw people racing track and field events on prosthetics in the Olympics. I saw one-legged skiers taking gates on the mountain. I saw people sit-down skiing on strange one-ski sleds. I was inspired and picked up the phone.

After leaving a message about being a new amputee from the war and interested in the 2003 Ski Spectacular, I was satisfied with myself for making the first step. The executive director, Kirk Bauer, called me back immediately. He was thrilled at my interest and told me that he was recruiting severely injured soldiers from Operation Iraqi Freedom for the event. He wanted me to come with six other soldiers and their families to Ski Spectacular as a special guest. That same night I spoke with the event coordinator, Kathy Celo, who coordinated the details for the event and asked me not to try to ski on my own. She said that she had the perfect instructor lined up for me and wanted me to wait for the event so that I wouldn't hurt myself and ruin the whole season.

It took another month before I got my doctor's approval, but he finally agreed that I was ready. I was in the best shape of my life. My physical therapist even put me on a strength-testing machine, and its report showed that my injured right leg was even stronger than my left. My therapist, Captain Dana Coval, pushed me to my limits. She was as dedicated to getting me into shape ahead of schedule as I was. The workouts were so painful that I had to ice down my leg and stump after each session. Some days, she was so intense that I couldn't keep up. She got me where I needed to be.

Mother Nature was making sure I wasn't tempted to go skiing by not giving us much snow during the month of November. The weekend before Thanksgiving, Kim, Forrest, and I drove up to Steamboat Springs to snowshoe out and cut down our own Christmas tree. That weekend was the first evidence to me that I was going to be able to ski. Even with the burden of the tree pulling on my shoulder harness, my snowshoes glided across the foot- to two-feet-deep snow. I found myself running with a new freedom I had not felt since before my injury.

■ ■ ■

I arrived at the Ski Spectacular on a Sunday, and in anticipation of the press that would be embedded at my lesson, I met my instructor to work out most of the adaptive portion of my preparation to ski. The instructor's name was Dave Callahan. Like most people I have mentioned, Dave and I have become great friends. There is something about the people I found myself surrounded by that I liked. Everyone helped each other and was committed to a single goal, and that was for all disabled people to overcome their disabilities. I loved the spirit and the people who lived it.

Dave was my kind of guy. After the normal introductions, he told me to get my gear on and get going. He was immediately confused as to why I wanted to ski on two legs, when it would be much easier and less painful to learn on one with outriggers. Outriggers are a type of ski pole with little skis that assist in turning and help you navigate down the mountain on one leg. Wanting to ski on two legs is a fight that adaptive instructors struggled with the whole season with our veterans. There is something mental about doing it whole, and we were all generally stubborn about learning the adaptive equipment. I didn't learn on one leg until I decided I wanted to teach it. So, immediately frustrated, Dave took me out to the snow. He figured that he should give me simple orders, like a soldier, because I might listen that way.

"Get those skis on, Captain. Let's ski down to the next lift to see where we are."

Although I said, "Okay," I thought, "You haven't even looked at my gear to see what may need to be adjusted."

But I did as ordered and hesitantly poled out to the open flat that led to the next lift. With my prosthetic leg, I had no ankle articulation and couldn't get my ski flat on the ground. I could not stand correctly. And I was on the best skis. After contacting the ski manufacturing company Rossignal, I was able to get the softest and most forgiving skis for my ability level, the Bandit B1. My skis wanted to go left, but when I tried to turn back to the right, I took a really hard fall. Embarrassed and frustrated, I picked myself back up and strained the rest of the way down the mountain.

Dave was waiting for me at the bottom and said, "Well, at least we know what the problem is. Let's go and get that boot wedged and adjusted."

We went to a ski shop and padded the inside of my Rossignal soft boots into a cant, an angled wedge, which then flattened my ski boot as I stood relaxed. Back on the snow, I felt almost like my old self again. I should have learned on one ski, as I was pretty much doing it anyway, trying to take the pressure off my throbbing stump. Regardless, by the end of the day, I was skiing on my own and going from the top of the mountain to the bottom.

Over a beer, Dave explained to me, "It's not your disability that's hindering your skiing now, but it's your bad habits from skiing before your injury that you need to work on. At least we know what you need to work on. Well, that and listening."

The next day, skiing with several different reporters and cameras, I took on the mountain. I was relieved that I had taken that hard fall and gotten it over with the day before the media arrived. I was proud and felt like I was living a dream after all those months on the couch.

After two days of skiing, I decided to try snowboarding again. Although I had only been snowboarding a few years, I was getting good and loved riding on big powder. I met with the Burton Snowboard Research and Development Team, who were in town testing boards, the night before snowboarding again. The team created a cant out of rubber for my right foot. I was unable to feel my stump, so the team also designed and made for me a stomp that was more like the foot stirrup you would use on a windsurfer. The stomp is a critical piece of equipment, because out of your bindings, it is where you put your foot while getting on and off the lift. Snowboarding again was so easy for me that I used my instruction time to learn to ride backwards. It was a blast, and another huge relief to know that this part of my life was not going to change. In fact, I was just getting better.

By the end of the week, I was in newspapers across the country and did a live interview with CNN. The highlight of the week was participating in a USSA certified Level II race alongside the U.S. Disabled

Ski Team. I didn't win the race, but I completed both my runs with competitive times. Most important, I raced.

Before my first run, someone asked me, "Are you nervous?"

I laughed and said, "Nobody is shooting at me, and I'm allowed to go as fast as I can on a closed course with perfect conditions. Are you kidding? This is killer!"

■ ■ ■

Skiing was back in my blood, but seeing what an effect it had on all the vets really made me take notice of its healing effects. Soldiers were showing up to the event embarrassed about their condition and a little apprehensive. By the end of the week, people found their sports. One realized that he had potential to be a great sit cross-country skier. Another who was missing both legs was determined to learn to ski standing up, but after some blisters decided to try the mono-ski (seated ski). Others also found a new confidence on their snowboards. Each person was enriched by the experience and left with a new confidence.

Kirk Bauer stood before us at the closing banquet and reminded us what we had accomplished during the week. He repeated the DSUSA motto: "If I can do this, I can do anything."

Those words rang in my head, and I thought about all the disabled soldiers coming back from the war. Before I left the event, I spoke with Kirk and Kathy Celo about what we could to do together to ensure that we could take care of every veteran we could. Kirk made it clear to me that he wanted to reach every veteran and get them involved in all the different chapters around the country, and even internationally. Kirk told me that he was going to send a message out to all the DSUSA chapters and ask them to give a free year of training and membership to disabled veterans from OIF and OEF. With that promise, I knew that we could get soldiers involved. I made a commitment to Kirk that I would do anything I could to help reach out to these soldiers.

It was less than a month before Kirk asked me to come and help him represent DSUSA at a ski event in Vail, Colorado, at which DSUSA would receive a check. My purpose was to show our fund-raisers how soldiers from the war could overcome their disabilities with the help and instruction of the program. It was at that event that I met Bill and Cheryl Jensen. Bill is the chief operating officer at Vail, and his beautiful wife, Cheryl, runs her own charitable organization.

When I met Bill, I thanked him for having me as his guest. He handed me his card and responded, "I believe in taking care of our veterans. If there is anything I can do for you, let me know."

I smiled and said, "I need nothing, but there are lots of veterans who need to be taken care of. We have a bunch of guys coming back more injured than I am who need to be part of events like this."

With an interested look he said, "You must meet my wife, Cheryl. She is interested in putting on an event at Vail."

Cheryl told me how she was working with Cheryl Barnes, executive director of the Wheelchair Foundation in Washington, D.C., who also wanted to do something for returning veterans. She explained that she wanted to put on a weekend for ten soldiers and their families, but was having a hard time getting access to soldiers to invite them. Problem solved. Through DSUSA, I promised her ten soldiers, and after losing a few to unexpected physical complications and surgeries, we had seven. Five soldiers were able to bring their families.

Each soldier had his own instructor; each instructor was paid out of donated funds. Each soldier stayed in a world-class resort donated by the local hotels. The highlight of the weekend was the dinner at the Vail Fire House. Since 11 September, there has been a unique relationship between firemen and servicemen. They put on a great spaghetti dinner and had lots of free beer. To top it all off, they were a great group of men. Again, each soldier left with renewed skills and the confidence that he could do anything.

It was my first event as a DSUSA representative. I was proud to be paying back what had become so important in my life. I officially became "Captain Dave." Kim and I both like the nickname, as it gives my due rank and also throws in the softer and more realized side of me. Although out of command in Iraq, I was part of something that seemed even more important. I was taking care of soldiers back home. Their interaction with me on the mountain may be the last memory they have of the Army. Those were my men. I was still training and leading. By seeing the soldiers learn and grow like they did, and seeing relationships renewed between husbands and wives, I really felt part of something great.

Most exciting was having NBC correspondent Kevin Tibbles along to document the entire four days. Although three minutes of footage on the *Today* show seemed short to me, considering the now personal subject, I know what a big moment in the spotlight it was. I also learned how important it was to create awareness. It is important for the American public to see how we overcome. These soldiers are proud to be injured veterans, and proud to have almost given their lives for something great. We renew athletics in athletic people and inspire them with the courage and confidence they need to go back out and take life by the horns. It is important for America to see that.

■ ■ ■

The renewed media attention brought on another wave of uncertainty. This time though, my doubt was whether I still wanted a career in the Army. I had a new mission, and that was taking care of amputees. It was something I felt I could definitely handle part-time and remain in the Army, but I was also confident that if I wanted to, I could make it a full-time career as a civilian.

Other job opportunities were shaping up as well. More civilian companies and some braches of government were recruiting me. I was flattered by all the attention and was feeling even more conflicted about my future.

The most frustrating part was that several political organizations were trying to convince me to run for public office. Some people felt I could succeed in politics because of my age, looks, confidence in speaking, and more. Plus, I really believed in something. They said, "Get out of the Army, head back to Texas, and let's get you elected in state government. In ten years, you'll be ready for politics in D.C. You want to make a difference? You can do it in Washington, and, David, you will. Give it a chance." Although I told them, "I just want to command troops," my head was spinning.

I talked to my friend Kirk Bauer and he made it quite clear. "As far as helping soldiers, you are. After you retire from the Army, there will still be plenty of time for you to help. I have no doubt that you can do anything you want. Choose what makes you happy." As for politics, he said, "In this city (Washington), people measure each other by their elected position. The more powerful you are, the more successful you are. What you need to do is define success for yourself."

■   ■   ■

I went to work trying to define myself, and the Army returned my call for help. After hearing about my volunteer interests on the news, the Fort Carson chain of command responded just as I hoped they would. Seventh Infantry Division Command determined that an amputee support group was necessary, and they wanted me to take a look at our systems at Fort Carson to make sure they were taking care of soldiers.

This new job was really an additional duty, as I was already back at work as the rear detachment regimental operations officer, and would soon take command of one of the rear detachments. As the operations officer, I was in charge of training and deployment of the replacements for the regiment. I willingly accepted the additional duty, as I knew that it would only help more soldiers.

My first recommendation was the one that was so important. I believed that I needed to make monthly visits to Walter Reed Medical Center. The only way to reach every soldier for support was to see every soldier. My suggestion was immediately approved, and within the week, I was off to Walter Reed for my first official visit.

I had two days to do a lot of work. The first day's intention was for me to visit the hospital wards, the Mologne House, which is the temporary lodging for soldiers at Walter Reed, and my surgeons and caretakers. The second day I planned on having Kirk Bauer join me to talk about what DSUSA was and what it was willing to offer every soldier.

It was a great honor to walk back into Walter Reed on my own two feet, even if one was new. As I entered the main entrance, I stopped to collect myself as I vividly recounted the last time I had been in that very spot, on my stretcher in the rain, 3 July 2003. It was at that moment that I realized how ready I was to visit and encourage soldiers, and just how important my new mission was.

My first stop was my temporary home while at Walter Reed, the dreaded Ward 57. The only place worse was the intensive care unit. Saying that you were on Ward 57 meant that you were going to live, but you were losing something. ICU meant that you might not make it at all. I proudly strolled into Ward 57 and immediately started visiting soldiers and the nurses and doctors who took care of me. Some didn't recognize me thirty pounds heavier, and others couldn't believe how well I was faking it. I wore my Class A uniform, because I wanted everyone to know that I was a decorated warrior from the 3rd Armored Cavalry Regiment and that I was still in the Army.

I saw one of my fellow captains, Mark Giammatteo, who had his leg destroyed by an RPG just weeks before. His spirits were shaky, but he seemed pleased to have a familiar face around. He was one of many brave soldiers I was able to visit with on Ward 57. You can't imagine the questions these guys carry around with them. I was glad that I had taken the time to sit down and write in my journal the questions and answers that these men shared with me. It was my aim to be their inspiration and provide testimonial for DSUSA based on my experiences at Ski Spectacular.

Although Ward 57 was an emotionally charged trip, catching the guys at the Mologne House was just as important. I was able to visit with a bunch of soldiers who were on their way out of the Army into the civilian world. It was the last chance for me to catch them before they had to find and contact DSUSA on their own, like I did. Even worse, in my mind, was having them go back and not know that any of these programs were available to them. We were able to sit down and informally talk over some issues and invite them to my briefing the following day. There were lots of questions asked, and many answers. This session was long overdue for some, and a fine end to an already successful day.

I can only describe the trip as a success. On a personal level, I got to come back to Walter Reed on two feet and show everyone that I had overcome. It was weeks later that I started to get feedback on my visits, but I received emails from doctors and providers who told me what a difference I was making. The hospital commander wanted to be sure that my command supported my visits, because he wanted me back as often as possible.

I wasn't aware at first how successful my visits were, because I didn't have a magic bullet to make the soldiers feel better. I just sat with them and talked to them. I would tell them my stories and show them pictures of my road to recovery. Sometimes I would pray with them, or tell jokes; it depended on the person. But everyone wants to be helped: It's just a matter of finding a way to their heart. I usually try to spend time with wives and families, as they are usually more prepared to ask questions. It was really important for mothers to see me up and around. My duty was to serve them, and I gave them all the time they needed. But two days was too short, and I couldn't wait for my next trip.

I didn't wait long. In March, I visited again, and it was just as memorable, or more. Since the last visit, I had completed my first sprint distance triathlon and was still skiing and snowboarding, so I had lots to show and tell. On the first day, I immediately went to Ward 57 to visit the more severely injured. After having had a few more months to heal, and the opportunity to participate in more races and events, I came better armed to talk to soldiers. It continues to amaze me what great spirits the men on these wards maintain. Even the most severely injured soldiers at Walter Reed have certain characteristics: determined, never quitting, hardworking, positive, and able. They are American soldiers, and are a symbol of hope for all amputees. Again, I was honored to make their acquaintance.

Besides spending most of the day in the wards, I was also able to spend some time with the soldiers in the pool doing hydrotherapy. Although I have become quite a swimmer, I was impressed with the level of therapy and cardio exercise that these single and double amputees are getting in the pool. It wasn't just the pool that impressed me about this visit to Walter Reed. Everyone was asking me to make sure to hurry back, as they were giving examples of soldiers who were inspired by me. They had learned from my and others' early experiences and had programs in place to better take care of soldiers.

As I returned a few times, I started to become friends with some, guys like Ryan Kelly and Heath Calhoun, to name a few. Ryan was a below-the-knee amputee and always took the time to thank me for spending time with him. Unselfishly, he would also make sure that I spent time with the guys who needed it most. These guys all shared the same spirit. Everyone looked out for each other.

Over a few too many beers one night, Heath, a double above-the-knee amputee, said, "Sir, you're awesome. I want to thank you for everything you do. I wish I could have fought with you in Iraq. I bet you were a great commander." He wasn't kissing my ass; he meant it. Little did he know that I would have thrown myself on a grenade for him any day. *He* was the one inspiring me. To hear that praise from just one guy makes it all worth it and kept me going back.

My last few visits have been about the same. I admit, it gets harder every time to go back and see severely injured soldiers. It's never easy to sit down with someone who is blind and missing both arms and a leg. But I keep going because it is important—for me and them. It has helped me heal, physically and mentally. By challenging those soldiers to stick with their treatment and therapy and prepare for the new world that I have discovered, I have become whole. Whether it was over lunch, at a sports event, in the ward, or helping in physical therapy, I was making a difference. I tried to set an example and offer hope. That is what these guys needed most.

CHAPTER 13

Fit for Duty

I N DECEMBER 2003, I DECIDED THAT it was about time to go
back to work. It was a difficult decision because I had a good
schedule and was comfortable. I was spending most of each day
helping other soldiers and I didn't want to give that up. But Kim was
tired of having me around the house all day on the phone and com-
puter, and was actually giving me hints that I needed to go back to
work. I was spending several hours a day either talking to soldiers,
helping to coordinate events for them, or putting veterans with similar disabilities in touch to help each other. I was just getting to the
point where I could wear my prosthesis through a hard morning
workout and still wear it the rest of the day. I wasn't sure how my leg
would do sitting behind a desk all day. I feared that I would reverse my
current success. Although work was becoming interesting to me, I was

completely dedicated to my physical recovery before starting a professional recovery.

It was really a battle in my mind, work vs. recovery. As if it were my new morphine, I needed to exercise every day. I was obsessed with my workouts, and carefully tracked my weight and strength gains in the weight room. It did not take me long to get my body to respond to the intense weight training. I went from being barely able to crutch from the car into the grocery store to swimming a mile in under forty minutes and bench-pressing over three hundred pounds. It actually took until almost April 2004 to get my body where I wanted it, but considering the starting point, I was extremely pleased.

I was even more critical of myself in the swimming pool. I wasn't able to swim until the end of September 2003, as it took that long for the thick, deep scabs on my stump to fall off. When I first tried swimming in the pool, I was participating in a community hydrotherapy class at the Fort Carson indoor pool. I felt like I was blowing through the balance and conditioning exercises, and on the second day I asked if I could end my workout with some lap swim. My physical therapist seemed pleased and recommended using a swim board to focus on my leg strength.

I pushed off the wall and started to kick hard with my good leg and splashed pitifully with my stump. I was turning right, straight into the wall. It was so embarrassing, but I kept trying. The only way I could go straight was to adjust with my right hand. But without my right hand on the board, I would lose the grip on it, and even hit myself in the face once as it popped free from my left hand. It was a mess and I quit halfway down the lane. I side-kicked back to the start of the lane and checked my watch. I has been told to swim for ten minutes, and I refused to quit. I decided to swim the crawl. I then swam about ten laps in the allotted time.

The first lap felt good. It was not at all awkward and I was able to make slight adjustments with my arms to go straight down the lane. Although I was going quite slowly, I was moving effortlessly. It was a freedom I had not felt in months, and I was joyous. Within weeks, I was swimming half a mile three times a week.

I continued to train my body and decided it was time to take an Army physical training test, which would be the next step to my recovery and return to the Army. The physical training test includes two minutes of push-ups, two minutes of sit-ups, and a two-mile run. All events are scored and graded on a scale broken down into age groups. Since I could not run, I chose one of the three alternate events, which include a choice of a 2.5-mile timed walk, 6.2-minute stationary bike, or a timed 800-yard swim. I chose the swim. With the DSUSA Ski Spectacular just a week away, and a doctor's approval to participate, I decided it was time to take the test. With little incident, and with Kim and Forrest cheering, I scored in the nintieth percentile for my age group in push-ups and sit-ups, and swam under the maximum time by two minutes. Another goal met.

With the physical training test under my belt, I went to visit the rear detachment commander to talk about a job. I felt a little brash going in to talk about work on my terms, but he was empathetic. I told him that I was ready to help the regiment again and wanted to get back to work. I explained how I intended to stay on active duty and was starting to feel able enough to accept my next command upon redeployment of the regiment. I was ready to work but could not commit myself full-time yet, as I needed to spend several hours a day working out and a few days a week at appointments. He admitted that he did not have a lot for me to do, but could put me on some special projects as the operations officer, which would offer me plenty of time to work out and attend all my medical appointments. Within a few months, he anticipated preparing the rear detachment for the regimental redeployment, and hoped that I would be able to come on board more fully. It was a great deal and a perfect reintroduction to the Army.

So there I was, back in uniform overseeing the training of the regiment's replacements. It felt good to work and to contribute to our success in Iraq. I think it was a bit daunting to some to have their last supervising officer before deployment stumbling around on a prosthesis, or some days, on no foot at all. More important, I was just back from the war and could share with them information that was going to keep them safe and alive. I was able to make contributions to training and certify leaders that were off to war. I felt like my participation was worthwhile and important to the regiment. I felt I still had value to the Army, and felt even more able to go back on active duty.

The only thing holding me back from being considered an active duty soldier again was my medical evaluation board. My status, "Recovering from Traumatic Injury, awaiting MED Board," made me uncomfortable. I hated seeing those words next to my name on briefings and memoranda that came across my desk. So, in typical fashion, I ran headfirst into the board process. I willingly went to the board and requested the board section to expedite the process because I wanted and needed to know if the Army would keep me. As the service usually had trouble with returning injured soldiers malingering on active duty, they were relieved to have a soldier who wanted everything to proceed rapidly. I finished all the necessary paperwork and medical examinations by the end of January. As my last submission, I was allowed to write a letter on my own behalf.

I had written it months before, in a period of conflict. I wasn't sure about what to do. "I think I've given enough," I told Kim the day I called her from the hospital in Baghdad. Had I? Was it time to move on from the Army? What was important to me now? I had a lot to weigh. Everybody—my soldiers, my commanders, my father—had high expectations for me. The Army had offered me a new command. I was a national media spokesperson for the service—how would it look if I quit? I felt strongly about duty to my country. But I also felt drawn to a new mission to help amputees. I also had to think about what was best for Kim and Forrest. I wrestled with it every day.

To answer those questions, I first had to know if the Army really wanted to keep me. I submitted this letter:

SUBJECT: Letter of Self-Recommendation and Fitness for Duty of Captain David M. Rozelle

1. I am capable and desire to remain on Active Duty in my assigned MOS. There have been no commanders back from the war to oversee my progress. All my success has been through self-discipline and self-motivated hard work. Therefore, I feel I have an obligation to myself to request my own retention. My chain of command has given me the flexibility to dedicate all of my recovery time to rehab and physical therapy. This confidence, as

well as my own personal motivation for retention, has already resulted in a dramatic recovery and rapid progress in my healing.

2. I was injured on 21 June 2003. My last surgery was 8 July 2003. I rushed the process and was on a prosthesis by 25 August 2003. In talking to amputee groups, I know that I am months ahead of most patients. I am completely dedicated to a full recovery. I am already considering my prosthesis an adaptive part of my body, which has no limits on me personally or professionally. Although I have, and will always have, a P3 profile for running, I don't believe that I will not be able to run two miles to standard within the calendar year. I feel that I have demonstrated my desire to maintain a level of fitness by passing an alternate PT test. I was in the gym and in the pool as soon as I was physically able. I am starting a "walk to run program" in January with my physical therapist, and should be running to standard within three to six months.

3. I believe that I will not be hindered in any way from performing all the tasks required of a cavalry officer. My future assignments do not include any physical activities that I cannot do now. I can fulfill all of the duties associated with my MOS, and am ready to prove them.

David M. Rozelle

CPT, AR

U.S. Army

As if to further convince myself to stick with the Army, the same week I finalized my medical board submission packet, I decided to participate in my first triathlon. I figured that if I could handle a triathlon,

I could handle Iraq again. My training partner in my spin class was actually the first to give me the idea. At first I thought she was being insensitive, but she was not. "Even if you walk the two-mile run, you will have finished a triathlon, which is a lot more than most people do," she said.

I thought about it for a few days. I kept in mind the DSUSA motto: "If I can do this, I can do anything." I registered.

It was a sprint-distance triathlon, which is a five hundred–meter indoor swim, an eight-mile mountain bike ride, and a two-mile run. For most, it is a gut check to see where you are in winter training and help you set goals for the summer triathlon series. By the end of the summer, you should be participating in Olympic distance races. Even the gut check seemed like more than I could do, but I set it as a short-term goal and trained for it. By the standards of my training regimen now, I am surprised I even made it out of the pool. But, like a typical rugby player, I made it through with brute force and ignorance. It was held on 28 February in Colorado Springs. It was a beautiful morning that felt more like spring than summer.

It was called the "Mid-Winter Chill Triathlon," but it didn't feel like winter when we all gathered at the pool and it was 75 degrees. I waited nervously for the last heat, as I had given a slow time estimate. As I dove in, the energy was there. I lapped each man in my lane at least three times. As I got out of the pool, I had to remember that I was in the slowest lane in the slowest heat in an attempt to not seem cocky. Truly, I had little to be cocky about, as I put up an eleven-minute swim time. (I can do that now in seven or less.) I felt much more confident on the bike and kept up with the lead pack most of the race. Then came the run. For my age group, I was putting up a pretty good score, and I think there was some concern among other racers about my foot speed.

The other runners were gathering up at the start line, and some were eyeballing me and my prosthesis. I guessed that these guys had seen paralympic runners on their carbon fiber springs blowing away records, and figured that I had a secret weapon. It probably didn't hurt their impression that I had recently developed such an athletic build.

As the other runners begin to crowd one another on the start line, they systematically pushed me to the rear.

I laughed and said, "Watch out, guys, this will be the fastest walking you have ever seen!"

One guy said, "Yeah, right."

Then the starter gave our start, and all looked back in disbelief as I started walking down the trail, whistling like some crazy old man. Completing the tri was my goal, and that is exactly what I did. I jogged about a third of it but did not push myself. The two miles I walked that day marked the farthest I had walked on my prosthesis since my injury. I was thrilled, and I was hooked—I knew I was going to do more triathlons.

As the race finished the snow was falling. The snow report for this front gave a prediction of twenty-eight inches in Beaver Creek. I knew some friends were coming into town at Vail, so I already had my snowboard packed next to my bike in the truck. As I went west in the mountains, the snow got deeper and deeper. By the time I got to Vail, the roads were closing and the pass was shutting down behind me.

It was the next day that my dream of fewer than three months ago came true. My dream was about skiing easily on the mountain without noticing my prosthesis, and it wasn't until I pulled up my pants leg and noticed my missing foot that I even thought about it. I had overcome it in my mind, and it was time for it to become a reality. As I traveled up the first lift, I shifted in my seat with the anxiousness of a child. There were no tracks. I was going to make fresh tracks in waist-deep powder the day after my first triathlon. I was giddy, whipping the chair like a horse, trying to make it get to the top of the mountain faster.

The moment my dream became a reality was such a short moment in time, but it was vivid. I had been surfing down through the powdered flats before I hit my first steep and dropped into a wide bowl. I made a tight S-turn and came back on an outcropping that I was able to take on my front edge and launch. As I grabbed for my toe edge, I inverted, and floated for a split second. That was the moment. Just like the feeling of freedom at the pool, I was flying. This time though, I was on a prosthesis and everything seemed back to normal. As I flew, I was not thinking about my injury or the limitations of my prosthesis.

I was flying, and screaming, "Yee-owww!"

I wish I could say that I landed that monster jump. After bouncing off my face, I did find myself back on my feet surfing up a natural bowl, and, just in case anyone was watching, did a little jump up on the ledge with a kick out. It wasn't until the bottom that I decided that it was the run of the day, even if it was my first. Any other run could ruin the memory of that perfect run. I sat in the snow eating some peanuts and drinking water, thinking about my run and the true freedom it brought me. I felt healed.

■　■　■

It was only a week later, on Kim's birthday, 4 March 2004, that my healing was confirmed and substantiated. I got a call from the Fort Carson medical evaluation board office. My case manager told me matter-of-factly to come by the office to pick up the results of the board. My heart fluttered with excitement and anticipation. Fortunately, Kim and Forrest also had appointments that day, so I met them at the hospital. As Kim finished up at immunizations with Forrest, I ran, and I do mean that I ran, upstairs to get my results. I found my case manager and took my file in hand.

It said it all in three simple words: "Fit for Duty."

I was elated. Then I was petrified. If I didn't want to proceed, I had seven days to appeal the board's ruling.

Now I had to decide. Now it was real. It had become easy to postpone this decision. In fact, I had almost expected the Army to take away the option for me. It would have made it easy for me to get out, and I would have had to submit an appeal to try to stay in. But that was irrelevant now. The Army wanted me. It had even moved me into a one-story "disabled" home to make my family and me more comfortable. Not only that, but I had become a poster boy for the service, and that created high expectations for me. I knew that even with the Army's decision, I could still get out. I had seven days to appeal. For the first time, I was afraid. Everything was set for me; all I had to do was accept. I had to ask myself one more time: Had I given enough? Where was my heart?

I put the decision off again. It was time to celebrate "Fit for Duty," not to make a final, difficult choice. The Army's ruling was a victory for me.

We had little time to think, as we had to get home and pack for our next event. The next day I was volunteering and participating in the Vail Disabled Veterans Weekend. I found myself again helping soldiers overcome their disabilities on the mountain, but this time as an officer with a certain future. For four days, I trained with Dave Callahan on my skiing and instructing. With such world-class instruction, I was skiing easily on one ski, and decided to learn the mono-ski. I knew that I would need to learn it eventually, as I intended to instruct it someday. Mono-skiing is skiing in its most pure form. It is almost like sailing. You can't force it, and you must let gravity and the fall of the Earth do all the work for you. It was incredibly challenging. I wore Dave out, as he constantly had to pull on the tethers to brake me and keep me upright.

By learning to mono-ski, I also wanted to continue to set an example for the soldiers. Everyone wanted to try stand-up activities, but I wanted the soldiers to see that it was rewarding to learn to sit-down ski. What they don't realize is that you are not always going to want to ski in your prosthesis, and it is nice to not miss a day of skiing because of sore stumps. Each night, I tried to represent Vail and DSUSA by taking care of the guys at different events. I tried not to act as a commander, but as a friend. But as the senior officer, I felt responsible for anything that happened. Fortunately, these young soldiers were too tired to cause any trouble, and we were all early to bed. It was another in a series of incredible weekends.

After another successful and rehabilitative veterans' event, I was back at Carson taking command of the rear detachment of the regimental headquarters and headquarters troop. It was not planned that I would assume the command of the troop right after getting word that I was fit for duty, but it was a great order of things. Even though

I was in charge of only a small detachment of staff and soldiers, we were the backbone of the redeployment of the entire regiment, well over six thousand soldiers. I went to work now with a renewed spirit and refreshed ideology of the Army.

I was selected to give the welcome-home briefs to the soldiers as they first hit the ground at Fort Carson. It was really a simple brief to welcome them back, fill them in on any new laws in Colorado, instruct them about the operations of their in-processing, and, of course, give them their safety brief for the long weekend ahead. As an amputee, I was proud to stand each day and give their briefings. It was a good testimony to each of them that the U.S. cavalryman can and will overcome all adversity. With such a volume of troops redeploying worldwide, it took almost a month for all the soldiers to get home. At each briefing, we celebrated the successes of the redeploying units and stopped to think about the soldiers who would never come home, but would never be forgotten.

After several weeks of briefings, and seeing lots of familiar faces, the Killer Troop men finally came home. I went early that day and rode out with the staff to greet the airplane at the Air Force base. I wanted to be the first to see my men. As soon as the stairs touched the side of the aircraft, I ran up and waited for the airline staff to open the door. As the door opened and was secure, I stepped aboard and stood face to face with Lieutenant Colonel Kievenaar. I gave him a big hug and found David Richkowski (Little Dave) waiting right behind him for his welcome. After exchanging more handshakes, I was ushered down the stairs and into the greeting line. I stood at the bottom of the stairs and surprised every one of my K Troopers.

All were happy to see me, and some were shocked to see me standing. Each had a thousand questions, but the receiving line was neither the time nor the place. I promised each of them that we would catch up as soon as I got them back to post. Most were satisfied, but took the time to give me a second hug or handshake to acknowledge me as being alive.

It was great to have my men home, but they were not home until they were with their families. Although my welcome-home ceremony was intimate, the Army has made a special effort to make these returning soldiers' homecomings special. In preparation for K Troop's return, I drove over and met Kim and Forrest at the Fort Carson Special Events Center, which is a gymnasium with a fancy name.

I must admit that I was a little jealous the first time I saw one of the welcome-home ceremonies. It was selfish of me to think that, as I enjoyed so many things while my men were deployed, but it is an incredible event. I had also become numb to it, as I had attended about twenty before K Troop came back. But this one was special, as I knew most of the wives and kids in the stands. Before the event started, I spent about ten minutes walking around hugging the ladies and kissing the kids. It was a night of celebration.

Events like these are the ultimate celebration of the Army's diversity. The bleachers that held the crowd were filled with every race and nationality you can think of. People had literally traveled the world to welcome their soldiers home. Most of the wives were dressed up. Some were eye-popping in their "wait until I get you home" outfits. My favorites were the kids with their fresh haircuts and new clothes. Lots of the little boys were in camouflage, and others were even in desert uniforms to match the soldiers. Everyone was happy. The building was alive with laughter and chanting. Each unit had banners up on the walls, and some families even held their own personalized ones. Some families had poster-sized pictures of their newborns so that as the soldiers entered they could find them in the crowd. As if there wasn't enough noise, the sound system was blaring patriotic pop songs, which some families were singing along with. No matter how you felt about the war, anyone would have found himself caught up in such a patriotic event.

As the soldiers came off the bus and formed outside, a new buzz traveled through the stands. As the four rows of doors opened, eight ranks of soldiers came marching in and formed, in military fashion, along the open floor. Three hundred tired soldiers stood facing a crowd that could not scream or clap hard enough. Kim was so overcome with emotion herself that I had to hold her.

To settle the crowd, the commanding general went to the podium and announced the soldiers' victorious return. After getting interrupted by the crowd's cheers, he addressed the soldiers to welcome them and then thanked the wives and families, who pay the true sacrifice. As is typical of any military ceremony, we saluted the flag and gave respect to the National Anthem. After the pomp and circumstance was complete, the commanding general ordered the commander of troops, which in this case was Lieutenant Colonel Kievenaar, to release the troops.

After saluting, Lieutenant Colonel Kievenaar turned to his soldiers and yelled out, "Prepare for the Regimental Accolade!"

All the soldiers in the building responded, "Prepare to sound off!"

Lieutenant Colonel Kievenaar: "Brave Rifles!"

Soldiers: "Veterans!"

Lieutenant Colonel Kievenaar: "Blood and steel!"

Soldiers: "AI-EE-YAH!"

Lieutenant Colonel Kievenaar: "Dis…missed!"

I backed Forrest's stroller well out of the way so he wouldn't be trampled by the crowd as the soldiers poured out onto the floor to find husbands and wives. There were people hugging and kissing, fathers crying as they held their babies for the first time, and proud mothers and fathers taking pictures of their sons and daughters. It was the happiest chaos you can imagine. One of my duties was to help families find their husbands and sons. It was that crazy. The sad cases are those soldiers who didn't have anyone to greet them, because of family problems or a family's inability to come. They immediately got my phone to call home and let someone know they were back.

I could now rest easy: Killer was back at Fort Carson. The only living person missing was Sergeant First Class McNichols. He had volunteered to act as the noncommissioned officer in charge of a boat guard detail and was not due for another month. Although I was lucky enough to not lose any men while I commanded K Troop, Killer did sustain two casualties over the remaining eight months of deployment in Iraq. My boys were back, and I was proud to walk through the crowd and see their smiling faces as they celebrated victory.

■   ■   ■

I remember driving home from the event. I was so proud to have my men back. I laughed about the memories I had of them at war. As I was driving near a firing range, I watched the tracers from small arms weapons burn as they flew down range. The sight reminded me that I was a cavalryman. I crested the hill thinking about all I had to do to get ready for my next command. I was excited to be working again. My starched uniform felt soft against my skin, and I thought about how comfortable it was. As I parked in the driveway, I pulled on my beret and checked to make sure it was straight in the rearview mirror. My captain's bars shined in the reflection and my face looked weathered. I thought, "This is who I am. I am an Army captain. A cavalryman. I love this job."

I had made my decision. I went on with my day.

■　■　■

After everyone was back, and my decision was made, I continued my duties for the regiment in support of the rear detachment. During that period, in the month of May, I found myself with more time, and I again focused on my physical training and assisting in special events for people with disabilities. In fact, I had done a lot in the last six months to help promote people with disabilities. It was almost like a second job. Besides becoming a national spokesperson for Disabled Sports USA, I had the opportunity to support several other events. Every now and then, I review my last year's calendar and am amazed at all I did. Just a few weeks after I learned to ski again, I was up in Steamboat Springs Powder Cat skiing with the Breckenridge Outdoor Education Center. The goal was to see if disabled people of all abilities could handle back-country deep-powder skiing. Talk about throwing me in the briar patch! Skiing again after the Vail event, I spent the week of 4–9 April at the Disabled American Veterans (DAV) event in Aspen. It was an event similar to the Ski Spectacular but was hosted by the DAV. Again, I worked with veterans, but this time as a mere participant.

Immediately following the DAV event, I participated as a disabled ski racer in the Breckenridge Outdoor Education Center's Snow Bash, which is an event to raise awareness and fund-raise for their disabled programs. It was a great way to spend Easter. I had a great time and enjoyed some of the best snow we had all year.

I also competed in a three-day Memorial Weekend bike race for Adaptive Adventures in Golden, Colorado. I am afraid the only awareness I helped with was the fact that I couldn't go pro on a bike anytime soon. It was a great event though, with a mountain stage race, a time trial track race, and a city sprint. It was the first time I had ever been part of a bike race. I was competing with the able-bodied pros, but the hand-cycle competitors raised the awareness. It was a blast and raised a lot of money for Adaptive Adventures. All of these events were fun and productive, and each helped me understand my disability better.

One of the most unique programs I've participated in was the Physical Fitness for Youth with Disabilities. I had no idea how out-reaching my mission would become. On 25 May, I flew to D.C. to participate in an awareness seminar with the Department of Health and Human Services. I was invited to be a guest speaker to talk about my injury and how I have not let it become a disability. The honor was mine as I sat and spoke to the large crowd, which was backdropped by our nation's Capitol. I spoke after Secretary Tommy Thompson and Surgeon General Richard Carmona. The children with disabilities from Catherine T. Reed School in Lanham, Maryland, sat in awe as I described the war, my injury, and road to recovery. Afterwards, watching the kids at the special activity exhibits, which included an obstacle course for wheelchair users, a climbing wall with adaptive equipment, table tennis, golf for people with disabilities, and even bowling for children with physical limitations, to include those who are blind, I felt a new sense of purpose. Kirk Bauer was always reminding me that we need to support all people with disabilities, but I had been so focused on veterans that it took this event to open my eyes to a new world.

A lot had happened since I first learned to ski, and I was participating in so much, but the triathlon season was now in full swing. Each time I competed, I got better and better, and still without my carbon spring foot. In July, I was at my physical peak and placed second in my division and third in my age group, against all able-bodied competitors. I was raising awareness at each event just by competing. I was inspiring not only disabled people, but I was now inspiring able people to better themselves.

■ ■ ■

It had been one hell of a year by the time I was able to take the troop colors back in my hand. I was ready to command troops again, but as a stronger and more mature leader. The history, traditions, and accomplishments of Remington Troop are embodied in its colors. They are passed from commander to commander as the command of the colors changes. In the history of the Army, the colors served as a rally point for soldiers during battle, and they now stood at my side to be carried back into combat. I am prepared again to die under the sway of the colors in the name of freedom.

I took command on 17 June 2004, just four days before the one-year anniversary of my injury, and two weeks before we received our next deployment orders to Iraq. Even with as much anticipation as there was for my return to command, the ceremony felt no different than my last.

But at the end of the ceremony, things became quite lucid.

I marched out in front of my troop, looked them over, did an about-face, and saluted with my report, "Sir, Remington Troop is formed."

As the regimental commander returned my salute, he smiled and ordered, "Troop Commander, take charge of your troop and prepare them for combat."

I recovered from the salute and shouted, "Brave Rifles!"

He responded, "Veterans!"

I did an about-face, beaming with pride, called my first sergeant forward and as I returned his salute, pride filled in me to my very soul. I was in command. My recovery was complete and I had met all my goals.

I smiled at him, holding my salute, and said, "Here we go again. AI-EE-YAH!"

Acknowledgments

There are so many to thank.

For all of you who have stopped me on the street and shaken my hand, hugged me in the grocery, sent me letters or presents, or bought me a beer, thank you for supporting the American soldier.

Mom and Dad, thanks for the "Word Drill!" Thanks to all of my family for your undying support.

Peter Barnes, you are a dear friend. Some of the greatest ideas occur on a cocktail napkin while sipping whiskey. Thanks for that glass of whiskey.

Kirk Bauer and Kathy Celo, from Disabled Sports USA, thanks for getting me back on skis. "If I can do this, I can do anything." *www.dsusa.org*

Thanks to the Challenged Athletes Foundation (CAF), who are committed to making the lives of people with disabilities better with every grant. *www.challengedathletes.org*

Brave Rifles to Marine Major Nico Marcolongo of Buddy Bowl, who holds a flag football tournament to raise money for injured soldiers and CAF. *www.buddybowl.org*

Thanks to Mary Bryant and Dick Traum of the Achilles Track Club, NYC, who tricked me into doing the New York City Marathon. *www.achillestrackclub.com*

Cheryl Barnes and the Wheelchair Foundation make dreams come true. *www.wheelchairfoundation.org*

Special thanks to Bill and Cheryl Jensen of Vail Resorts and the Vail Veterans Weekend, who are touching soldiers' lives.

Thanks to Breckenridge Outdoor Education Center, who give such fabulous support during Ski Spectacular and beyond. *www.boec.org*

Thanks to Sergeant First Class McNichols for allowing me to lead from the front and then for dragging me out of the minefield.

I want to thank the Army for finding me "Fit for Duty." I will not let you down.

Thanks to Colonel Teeples and Lieutenant Colonel Kievenaar (and family) for believing in me and offering me a second command.

Thanks to Colonel H. R. McMaster for trusting me to take soldiers back to war. Brave Rifles.

Thanks to all the doctors and nurses in Bagdhad, Landsthul, and Walter Reed Medical Center. Your care is second to none.

Thanks to all the amputees out there who have allowed me to be their voice. I will always represent you for what you are, heroes.

Thank you, Mr. President, for your personal encouragement in our meetings and correspondence. Your leadership is steady and decisive. Your men are honored to serve you and this great country.

To God, whom I serve, thank you for saving me.